# BEYOND

# RACISM

BUILDING AN OPEN SOCIETY

BY **Whitney M. Young, Jr.**

McGRAW-HILL BOOK COMPANY

NEW YORK   TORONTO   LONDON   SYDNEY

I am particularly anxious to acknowledge the invaluable and essential role of Daniel S. Davis, who unselfishly bore the major editorial responsibility for this book.

This book is dedicated to my parents. With eternal grati-
tude to my father, Whitney M. Young, and to the memory
of my mother, Mrs. Laura Ray Young.

# CONTENTS

INTRODUCTION
## THE OPEN SOCIETY
(1)

CHAPTER ONE
## BLACK AMERICA
(15)

CHAPTER TWO
## WHITE AMERICA
(71)

CHAPTER THREE
## BUILDING AN OPEN SOCIETY
(149)

CHAPTER FOUR
## RESPONSIBILITY FOR CHANGE
(203)

# BEYOND

# RACISM

# INTRODUCTION

# THE OPEN SOCIETY

Our nation is moving toward two societies, one black, one white—separate and unequal.

Discrimination and segregation have long permeated much of American life; they now threaten the future of every American.

—REPORT OF THE NATIONAL ADVISORY COMMISSION ON CIVIL DISORDERS

AMERICA IS poised at the brink of disaster. We are caught in the clutches of a racial crisis of such overwhelming proportions that the very future of democracy is at stake. The course this nation charts in the coming months will determine whether we shall finally achieve our long-lost goal of a democratic nation of equals or descend into the maelstrom of police-state repression.

It is easy to ignore the warning signals. People have become hardened to crises and predictions of doom. The past thirty years have seen a great depression, a cataclysmic world war, two bitter Asian land wars, and a prolonged cold war—all of them accompanied by warnings of danger. Americans are used to sitting on the knife-edge of disaster.

But the present crisis is like no other. It comes not from external enemies nor from economic forces, it comes from within ourselves. Its roots are deep within our own history and its resolution depends not on the next turn of the economic cycle or building bigger armies, but on our ability to change our own actions and our own thought patterns.

The racial whirlwind has been gathering for a long time, but only when riots swept nearly every city of any size in America did people finally understand that we are caught within a national agony to find a parallel for which we would have to go back over a hundred years, to the Civil War.

Even now, after the publication of the Report of the National Advisory Commission on Civil Disorders and the multitude of television "specials" on ghetto conditions, many

Americans refuse to face the seriousness of the racial crisis. With typical optimism, they assume that it will settle itself, or perhaps that it will just go away. It won't.

The word *crisis* itself has been so overused and misapplied to other situations that it no longer has the emotional weight the current situation demands. The dictionary provides several definitions of *crisis,* but the one perhaps most applicable to our current state is "the point in the course of a disease at which a decisive change occurs, leading either to recovery or to death."

The message is clear: the sickness of racism has brought our nation to the point where its most cherished values, indeed its very essence, will die, or it can overcome the sickness which is sapping its life and recover to a state of racial health, equality, and justice.

When written in Chinese, *crisis* is composed of two characters; one represents danger, and the other represents opportunity. It is the purpose of this book to explain the dangers inherent in our racial crisis, and to show the exhilarating opportunity it offers Americans to build the first society in the history of the world that is truly open and alive with possibilities for all men of all races.

The fate of all Americans is inextricably tied to the fate of black Americans. America has relentlessly persecuted black people for 350 years, in the process creating a second America, separated geographically and psychologically. The American version of apartheid has walled blacks into racial ghettos, kept them from the best jobs, given their children the worst education. Every day 25 million blacks are reminded in dozens of ways, large and small, that they constitute an inferior caste within the nation that boasts of being the leader of the "free world."

But because of the enormous population shifts that have taken place, this historic mistreatment of blacks has been transformed from a blot on the national conscience into a threat to the very existence of this urbanized nation. Three out of four Negroes once lived in rural areas; now three out of four live in cities. Massive migrations from the South, still continuing at the rate of more than 80,000 people a year, have turned black people into city-dwellers and the cities into black enclaves.

Between 1940 and 1960 the black population of metropolitan areas more than doubled, and by 1985, if present trends continue, it will double once more. Within a generation at least eleven major cities will join Washington, D.C., and Newark in having black majorities. Cities as diverse in geography and character as Chicago and Jacksonville, Atlanta and Detroit, Gary and Philadelphia, Baltimore and Oakland, and St. Louis, Cleveland, and New Orleans will all have one thing in common: the majority of their people will be black. And many other major cities will have Negro minorities of a third or more.

Here too, discrimination has played a leading role; migration and natural increase would not be enough to turn the cities into vast black ghettos. It took the flight of middle-class whites into rigidly segregated suburbs to make the above figures possible. Between 1950 and 1965, New York City lost the incredible total of 1,500,000 white people, most of them to the suburbs ringing the city. In the same period, these mostly middle-class whites were replaced by about 1,250,-000 Negroes and Puerto Ricans of lower educational levels and income.

This population shift places black people in potential political control of the very heart of our national power. The historic America of yeoman farmers and gentry is long dead, if indeed it ever existed. The metropolis is the center of America today. It holds the seat of our government, the offices of our corporations, and many of the jobs, services, and schools upon which the nation depends.

Continue to populate these cities with the poor, the angry, the rejected, and they become repositories of social dynamite.

Our cities are already virtually bankrupt because of the exodus of middle-class whites and the mushrooming demand for costly social services required by the impoverished slums. New York's slums cost well over $3 billion—half of that for welfare alone. There are close to one million people on the welfare rolls of that city—a dependent population large enough to be the nation's sixth largest city.

St. Louis is a perfect example of the fiscal straitjacket the cities find themselves in. Since 1950, a quarter of a million people left the city, while the black population, now 40 per cent of the total, doubled. Manufacturing employment declined by a quarter. Unemployment in the black ghetto hovers around 10 per cent, with twice that percentage working in part-time or marginal jobs. The median family income is less than half that of the surrounding suburbs. But the tax rates are higher: in 1966 the city squeezed an average of $254 from each of its residents while the affluent suburbs averaged only $153 per head.

But the city can barely cover the costs of the festering slums. Hospital costs and health services cost the city $34 for each of its citizens, but the suburbs spent only $8 for each of their healthy middle-class residents. Police protection cost the city $32 per capita, the suburbs $10. The costs of poverty, crime, and bad housing ate up whatever the city could spend—and its children paid for it. St. Louis spent only $86 per person on its schools, the affluent suburbs $117. This case history in the deterioration of a city is repeated in almost every city in the United States.

And this already disastrous situation will worsen. If Negroes continue to be concentrated in marginal jobs, the unemployment rate for black workers in 1975 will be around the 20 per cent mark. The Commerce Department estimates that twenty-five of the largest metropolitan areas will have a shortage of nearly 3 million jobs in that year. The increase in the labor force, especially in the young labor force fifteen to forty-four years of age, makes it imperative that we take immediate steps to create new jobs and restructure our economy. The National Commission on Urban Problems, headed by former Senator Paul Douglas, estimates an increase of startling proportions in this age group in metropolitan areas by 1985: 67 per cent more white workers and *129 per cent* more black workers!

The very fact of racial concentrations of black people relentlessly segregated into impoverished, overcrowded ghettos is itself explosive. It leads to a "we-them" attitude, emphasizing the "apartness" of the isolated group. It sets in motion feelings of hostility and suspicion leading to irrational acts that endanger us all. The sense of imprisonment in an atmosphere of externally imposed inferiority results in unbearable tensions within the ghetto, tensions that explode in riots and violence.

Behind the ghetto's cry for self-determination is the knowledge that it is controlled largely by white institutions that historically have been totally unresponsive to the needs and aspirations of black people. The poverty that stalks black America is the direct result of the premeditated exclusion of blacks from the jobs, schools, and housing reserved for white people. Unless we can devise ways to admit black people to full participation in the social, political, and economic life of the larger society, the bitterness and despair of the impoverished black masses will bring about the destruction of the cities.

This was basically the message of the National Advisory Commission on Civil Disorders (the so-called Kerner Commission, for its chairman, then-governor Otto Kerner of Illinois). The Commission was created in July 1967 by President Johnson after some of the worst riots in American history. The Commission consisted of relatively conservative individuals; the spectrum of political ideologies ran from moderate conservative to liberal. Only two Negroes were appointed—Republican Senator Edward W. Brooke and NAACP executive director Roy Wilkins. The remainder of the panel was drawn from Congress, state and city officials, business and labor. The presence of such men as industrialist Charles B. Thornton, Ohio congressman William M. McCulloch, Atlanta police chief Herbert Jenkins, and United Steelworkers' president I. W. Abel insured that the panel could not be stampeded to acceptance of extreme viewpoints. Its members were the embodiment of cautious prudent opinion. And yet, the Report it issued was unique in that it gave the sanction of a presidential commission to what many knew all along but few dared to say—that we are moving toward separate and increasingly hostile societies; that the cities are in a state of extreme crisis, and that the future of the country is at stake.

What happened? According to news reports, the first meeting of the Commission was spent discussing the presumed role of provocative agitators in fomenting the riots. But then they listened to witnesses; they went into the ghettos; they climbed the broken stairways of decaying tenements; they saw the rat bites on children with bellies swollen with hunger; they heard the anger and frustration of men who couldn't get jobs. They saw at first hand what America does to its poor and its blacks, and then they wrote a Report few of them could have imagined signing a few short months before.

Their experience wasn't that unusual. It was repeated in Jackson, Mississippi, where the mayor told Negro leaders at a meeting of the city council "There are no slums in the city of Jackson." Two days later he was taken on a tour of the black ghetto of the city of which he had been mayor for twenty years. He emerged shaken. "I've seen things today I wouldn't have believed existed," he confessed.

Like most white Americans, he suffered from the social blindness that prevents them from seeing the problems of black people and from doing anything about them. But, thanks to the Kerner Report, some people had their vision restored in 1968. And others were shocked to new understandings because of the tragic deaths of Dr. Martin Luther King, Jr., and Senator Robert F. Kennedy. The murders of these apostles of reform led many people to rededicate themselves to fight for the ideals for which these men laid down their lives.

In many other ways, 1968 was a crucial year in the war against racism. Black Americans evidenced a new spirit of determination and an awareness that the obstacles white America has placed in the path of black people can only be overcome by the unified action of a black community determined to be free, and single-minded in its efforts to achieve equality.

The business community finally woke up, too. America's responsible business leaders finally understood the threat to prosperity posed by the ghetto, and through the actions of individual companies or through new structures like the Urban Coalition and the National Alliance of Businessmen took new steps to reverse the historic exclusion of black workers from industry.

Yet another hopeful sign is the resurgence of democratic values among young people. The so-called generation gap has many features, but one of the most important lies in the questioning of adult morality. Young people just won't buy the hypocrisy and the racism they see in their elders. They know the ghetto exists—they dance to its music and sing its songs. Their colleges are often located on the fringes of urban misery. They are the best-educated generation in our history, and their idealism and honesty lead them to reject the split-level values of their parents. They don't think a second color television set is the aim of life, and they can't see the virtues of expense-account cheating—and they can't tolerate racism.

These are new and encouraging elements of hope, but the basic problems remain, and they have even worsened. Congress continued to starve important social programs, and the discontent of the insecure working and middle-class whites has led to increasing polarization. Alabama's ex-governor George Wallace found alarmingly large numbers of supporters for his message of hate in the urban north, and many white neighborhoods on the fringes of ghettos came to resemble armed camps.

The urgency of our racial dilemma has yet to be fully understood by the majority of white Americans. Perhaps one in ten is fully committed to transforming society, and perhaps another one in ten is actively committed to hate and racism. But the great mass of Americans suffer from indifference; they have no conception of the dangers we face or even of the conditions their indifference has fostered.

They don't understand the truth of the words Robert Kennedy uttered to an audience of South American students, words that clearly spell out the dominant message of our era: "The responsibility of our times is nothing less than a revolution . . . We can affect its character; we cannot alter its inevitability."

The present racial tensions raise the question of the very survival of our urban society. A social revolution will come, but we can insure that it is peaceful and creative. Mass rioting and rigid repression leading to a fascist police state are both unacceptable alternatives.

The revolution of our times must be one which creates an Open Society. The vision of an Open Society is one that can be shared by all decent people of whatever color. It is a vision of an America in which children don't go hungry because their skin happens to be black, an America in which men don't go jobless because their skin happens to be black, an America in which mothers don't go homeless because their skin happens to be black.

It is a vision of an America that glories in diversity and respects the unique contributions and traditions of all of its people. An Open Society will bring whites and blacks together in true equality, eliminate poverty, restore the cities to greatness.

The institutional and behavioral changes that will make the Open Society a reality will come about when both blacks and whites are galvanized to change our present society. I recall the Jules Feiffer cartoon that shows a worried-looking young man saying over and over again, "We're a sick society. We're a sick society." Finally a girl comes up to him and says "Instead of talking about it, why don't you do something to change it?" At that, he straightens up and says "We're not all that bad, we're not all that bad."

But this *is* a society that suffers from the sickness of racism, a society torn by deep-seated tensions and urban rot. It won't be changed until the decent people stop talking about it and start working to create a new and better society, one in which all Americans can choose their way of life and exercise the options within a democracy.

Basically, it is up to each of us, white and black, rich and poor, to transform our country. Institutional changes are vital, but each individual can become involved by doing specific things, and starting right in the home. You, the reader, will find a checklist for action in Chapter 4; to a degree far greater than we may realize, the future of America may depend on what you do about it.

"A house divided against itself cannot stand," said Lincoln. And now, a hundred years later, the house of democracy is still rent by division. Black people aren't going to solve the problem by moving back to Africa or retreating into some fantasy-world of a separate state. We are Americans; our forefathers' blood, sweat, and tears watered every blade of grass, every inch of land of this country. America belongs as much to the black man as to anyone else. America's wealth was built by slave labor and, later, by the ruthless exploitation of the black caste which was denied its fair share of the wealth it created.

The two Americas must realize that the fate of each is tied to the other. We can work together to create an Open Society which brings dignity to all men, or we can die together in an agony of hate and violence. The choice is ours.

# CHAPTER ONE

# BLACK AMERICA

Segregation and poverty have created in the racial ghetto a destructive environment totally unknown to most white Americans.

—REPORT OF THE NATIONAL ADVISORY COMMISSION ON
   CIVIL DISORDERS

BLACK AMERICA was created in slavery and took shape over another hundred years of oppression. It is "another country," in the midst of our cities as well as in the countryside. Black America is the rundown tenement in Harlem, the sharecropper's shack in Mississippi, and the neat bungalow in Watts.

Black America is now forging its own identity from its own experience. "Black is not a color of the skin," writes actress Ellen Holly. "It is a unique experience shared by Negro Americans, however varied they may be, that sets them apart from any other group and results in a certain kind of psychological adjustment that no other group has to make —namely, the adjustment of learning how to survive, and perhaps even to flourish, in an atmosphere that is almost totally hostile."

Few white Americans understand the depth of the hostility black people face, or the sheer effort blacks have had to make simply to survive. Other groups have met with discrimination but no other minority, with the exception of the American Indian, has been so totally relegated to the farthest corners of American life.

One of the questions most often asked is "We made it, why can't they?" Nearly every nationality group in the American melting pot cherishes a newly won middle-class status, erecting myths of the perseverance of immigrant ancestors who, unaided, wrested wealth and respectability from an America willing to reward hard work. "Negroes must be lazy," many whites conclude; "black people want it handed to them on a platter, while we had to work for what we got."

No, Negroes aren't lazy. Black men worked and died building America. They worked from sunup to sundown in the fields of the South while their white masters sipped mint juleps in the shade. They built the railroads of the South, and everywhere did the dirty work in the hardest jobs—jobs that white people considered beneath them. Even today, black people perform the grueling stoop labor on the farm, the pick-axe laboring work in the cities. They do the housework and the laundry, and fill a host of other insecure, ill-paid jobs white people won't touch. When Ford and the other auto-makers announced that they would hire 6,500 unemployed workers for factory jobs, 14,000 blacks lined up in front of the unemployment offices before they opened. No, blacks aren't lazy; and if they have learned anything from their experience in America, it is that no one will hand them anything on a platter.

But blacks haven't "made it," while other groups have, and the reasons are no less real for being complex.

The great waves of immigrants reached these shores at a time when America was underpopulated and the virgin lands of the West were still open to settlement. Land agents plastered Europe with recruiting posters to attract settlers. When the immigrants arrived here, the government turned over to them tracts of fertile land, provided them with low-cost loans to buy equipment, and then taught them how to cultivate their land.

Those who stayed in the cities found laboring jobs plentiful. All that was needed here were a strong back and a willing mind. Men could go into business: there was room for a host of small enterprises servicing the ethnic community. Of course, they met with discrimination, but they could still get jobs at decent pay, and as their numbers increased prejudice gave way to grudging tolerance, and finally to acceptance.

Immigrant groups found ethnic communities already established, which had institutions that helped them to adjust. Jewish immigrants from Eastern Europe found a well-established Jewish community, which included many rich individuals and a tradition of philanthropy. Irish and Italian immigrants were helped by the Catholic church and Catholic relief agencies.

Those who settled in the cities quickly became a political force, catered to and serviced by the big-city political machines. The traditional Christmas basket was just one of a whole range of services that included jobs, recreational facilities for children, and help in dealing with landlords and city agencies. Eventually some of these groups, such as the Irish in Boston, took over the city government from the hostile Yankee patricians.

And it didn't happen overnight. The immigrant father didn't throw away his shovel to work in his son's law office. It took several generations of slow but steady advancement. Children left ethnic enclaves, and their children went on to college. Some changed their names, but all found that they had the choice of remaining hyphenated Americans or of melting into the landscape of white America, virtually indistinguishable from their neighbors. The war and the postwar economic boom catapulted most ethnic groups into middle-class prosperity and full acceptance.

But the black American, who was here before the *Mayflower,* was left behind.

## BEYOND RACISM

When boatloads of European immigrants were being settled on fertile lands in the expanding West, the black man was tied to the Southern soil in a state of peonage. Legally free, he was in fact as enslaved as ever. Those in the cities saw the few jobs open to them disappear as white employers preferred whites. Even before the Civil War, Frederick Douglass was moved to write of free Negroes in the North: "Every hour sees us elbowed out of some employment, to make room perhaps for some newly arrived immigrants, whose hunger and color are thought to give them a title to especial favor."

Slavery left black people without the strong family structure immigrants found so vital. Black men saw their wives sold, and black mothers lost their children on the auction block. While tightly knit European families were working together, black people were just beginning to build the institution of the family.

By the time black people became immigrants themselves, moving northward to settle in the cities, they found a totally different economic environment. Strong backs were no longer needed—machines did the heavy work. Job requirements changed: education was the key to economic success and the schools of the South had been geared to providing farm laborers, not engineers or scientists.

The black man was caught in a technological revolution. The unskilled labor, which gave other groups an economic foothold, was no longer needed, and the highly paid skilled trades were locked up tight behind a WHITES ONLY sign. The small businesses, the economic lifeline of other groups, became outmoded in an age of chain stores and shopping centers. The political machines, which helped sustain other groups with jobs and favors, were largely rendered powerless by reform government and civil service. Poor education and prejudice kept blacks out of the white-collar office jobs which were the new stronghold of the emerging middle classes.

But the black migrant differed from his predecessors in the city in yet another, more crucial way. He was black. The black man could not change the color of his skin and melt into the white background. He couldn't simply correct an accent or change a name to avoid discrimination. He found himself at the mercy of an economic and social system that excluded all blacks, and there was nothing, absolutely nothing, he could do himself to win an equal chance.

Whatever grudging concessions the system was willing to make for European immigrants, it absolutely refused to grant them to the black man. The earlier immigrants may have realized that their ten-hour day of ditch-digging or sweatshop labor would not result in riches for themselves, but they had ample evidence that their efforts would pay off for their children. They knew that the system was open-ended and that whatever they scraped together for a son's education would pay off in his freedom, if not their own. The black worker labored as hard, but he knew that he could only hope to bequeath his shovel to his son; he knew the system was closed, and that a black man dared not hope.

In the face of this, the real question that should be asked is not "Why haven't Negroes made it?" but "Why have so many Negroes made it?" It is a testimony to the perseverance of black citizens, and to their abiding faith in an America that systematically persecuted them, that so many black people have wrenched a measure of success from their hostile surroundings.

But times are changing. The more overt forms of repression are being neutralized by the various civil rights laws of recent years and by the growth of a more civilized attitude about racial matters on the part of growing numbers of white Americans, and now black men are no longer willing to tolerate their third-class status.

The black man today is fully aware of his inferior status. He knows that it is man-made, not God-given. He is no longer isolated in the rural backwaters of our country, dependent upon local feudal plantation-owners for his news of the outside world. He has the same access to radio, newspapers, and television as whites. He has had enough contact with whites to appreciate the good things in life they take for granted, but he also has enough contact with whites to be aware of the hypocrisy, the corruption, and the moral rot that pervades society. He no longer looks up to the white person and to white society as models to emulate.

Black people are no longer satisfied with the crumbs from the white man's table. The black man knows that his blood, sweat, and tears are on every dollar bill that pumps our giant economy—an economy that relegates him to the bottom of the ladder in jobs, in income, and in all areas of life. The black man wants his share of America—and he wants it now. He's had promises for 350 years; now only results will do.

This is hard for many whites to understand. The white person sees some very dramatic gains Negroes have made in the past several years. He sees black men in a variety of jobs they never held before. He even sees black men in government, the Senate, and on the Supreme Court. He reads about the expanding black middle class, and he may even take more notice of the new cars he sees driven by blacks or the expensive suits worn by some black acquaintances. But what he sees are the absolute gains made by some blacks. They are the visible top of the iceberg; hidden from his view are the ghetto masses whose lives have been relatively untouched by the slight changes that have taken place. While some blacks have made measureably significant gains, so, too, have most whites, and the position of black citizens relative to whites is only slightly changed.

Black America is an economic disaster area. The booming American economy, so generous in its rewards to white citizens, short-changes black workers. Median family income for whites rose to a record $8300 in 1967, but for blacks it was $4900. Fifteen years ago black income was 57 per cent that of whites; in 1967, after the most prolonged period of prosperity in our history, it crept up only two percentage points, to 59 per cent.

These figures gain even greater impact when you understand that Negroes are city-dwellers and urban life is far more costly. According to the U.S. Bureau of Labor Statistics, a city family must earn $9191 to maintain a "moderate" living standard—in New York it's $10,195. So black families make barely half what they need to live adequately in the American city. Most families who *do* make it past the $10,000 mark are unable to do so on one salary alone—in three out of four of these families, wives work. Less than half the wives in white families in that income bracket have to work.

Although every tenth American is black, black people make up a third of the nation's 26 million poor. And the income gap in the cities is even more shocking: only one in twenty urban white families with children is poor compared to every fifth black urban family with children.

Unemployment for black workers is more than double that for white workers, and has been since 1954. When the U.S. Labor Department made a special survey of employment patterns in the ghettos of six major cities, it found that up to half of ghetto workers were unemployed or underemployed.

Official America has masked the disastrous impact of black unemployment by emphasizing the myth that the nation has "full employment" because our over-all unemployment rate is under 4 per cent. But no other industrial country in the world is satisfied with 4 per cent unemployment; in Japan and Sweden and West Germany the norm is 1 per cent. Four per cent in the U.S. means more than 8 per cent for black workers, and that doesn't include the underemployed—people who are working part-time or full-time for less than poverty-level wages—nor does it include the many who have simply given up in despair and dropped out of the economy. Another myth, quite popular these days, is that when unemployment drops below 4 per cent, inflation becomes a problem. In effect, that means letting Black America pay for White America's price stability. Better hungry black kids than less purchasing power for an already sated middle class!

The figures also hide the impact of unemployment on the ghetto. Rosy national figures don't tell of the one out of four black teenagers who can't get jobs, compared with only one out of ten white teenagers. The figures may show that Cleveland, for example, has a 3.5 per cent unemployment rate, but they don't show that the Hough ghetto in Cleveland has a rate five times as high.

But unemployment alone is not the reason for black poverty. Black people with jobs are poor too. Roughly a third of all poor families are headed by a person who has a full-time job. Black workers are disproportionately concentrated in the lowest-paying jobs; they hold one out of every four low-wage jobs.

Black workers doing the same work as whites pay a color tax: they get less pay. The Chicago Urban League did a study of unskilled workers in Chicago that documents this discrimination. The average black worker in the study had more education, more time on the job, and had lived in Chicago longer than the white workers in the study. But the average weekly wage for the black worker was $55.56—almost $10 a week *less* than the white worker got. The Census Bureau's Herman P. Miller estimates that black factory workers earn a third less than whites, and black truck drivers and deliverymen earn 42 per cent less.

Education has been enshrined by Americans: "Go to college and you'll get a good job." *But blacks who have attended college earn less than white high school dropouts.* And a U.S. Senate report released in 1968 documents a $1140 gap between black college men and white high school graduates. Part of the reason for these figures is the fact that discrimination often leads black college graduates into safe but low-paying jobs such as teaching or the clergy, in contrast to relatively less well-educated whites who can get top-dollar jobs in the skilled trades.

A lot of this is changing. White colleges are wooing black students, and personnel recruiters at some of the smaller black colleges sometimes threaten to outnumber the students —everybody is looking for an "Exhibit A" to integrate the headquarters and staff. But despite these changes, white-collar really means *white*. The Equal Employment Opportunity Commission made a survey of white-collar workers in nine major cities and found, to no one's surprise, that black workers weren't getting office jobs. In Atlanta, where Negroes make up a fourth of the metropolitan area's population, blacks had only 2.3 per cent of the white-collar jobs; in New Orleans, with a third of the population, blacks held 3 per cent of these jobs—in all of the cities surveyed, blacks held a minuscule number of white-collar jobs and were concentrated in the blue-collar job sector.

And these blue-collar jobs are fading in importance. About as many people work in factory production jobs now as twenty-five years ago. Technology is eliminating these jobs and at the same time creating new jobs in sales, finance, and other areas from which blacks have traditionally been excluded. Inadequate education, unrealistic testing and hiring procedures, and overt discrimination keep the ghetto worker locked into marginal, low-pay jobs.

This situation is going to get worse. Young black workers will enter the labor force of the 1970s at a rate double that of white workers. And, unless job discrimination ends and housing patterns change, they won't be able to get jobs, and America will truly find itself in a revolutionary state.

## BLACK AMERICA

Few people understand how housing segregation, bad education, and job discrimination work hand in hand to keep black workers from their share of America's jobs and income. The new jobs are being created in the suburbs, which remain mostly lily-white. Between 1954 and 1965, about two thirds of all new industrial buildings went up outside the downtown areas, as did half the new stores. A Rand Corporation study says that there will be a 20 per cent shift in employment from city to suburb by 1975, and that 56 per cent of jobs in metropolitan areas will be in the suburbs.

The 1967 report of the U.S. Commission on Civil Rights describes a classic example of this city-suburb job squeeze:

The city of Oakland—in Alameda County—has a population of 385,700. About 120,000 are non-white. The unemployment rate for the Negro population was 13 per cent; another ten per cent of the male working force was neither working nor looking for work; the unemployment rate for teenagers was 41 per cent. Yet, in suburban portions of Alameda County—where there are approximately 185,000 jobs at all skill levels—only a small fraction, roughly 3,700, are held by Negroes.

Few Negroes live in suburban Alameda County. Public transportation from central city to suburban areas is limited and expensive and the cost of commuting by car . . . is more than most slum residents can afford. Employers, moreover, prefer to hire persons living close to work in order to reduce absenteeism and to build a labor pool which can be recalled easily after layoffs.

A short drive through the new roads of burgeoning suburbia will take you past dozens of new factories, shopping centers, and industrial parks, as well as through pleasant new housing developments. This is the heartland of White America. You won't find many black faces behind the counters, at the machines, or in the back yards of the affluent gilded ghettos white Americans have created for themselves.

Cities such as Philadelphia and San Francisco have doubled their black populations since the war, but the percentage of blacks living in the suburbs that surround them has *actually decreased*. More than a fifth of all city-dwellers are black, but barely a twentieth of suburbanites are black. And even those figures are misleading, for they don't truly reflect the extent of America's apartheid, since many blacks in the suburbs are crowded into mini-ghettos far removed from the broad tree-lined streets and ample lawns of their suburban neighbors.

The cities themselves, as they become blacker, are becoming more segregated. Karl Taeuber, a sociologist, examined the degree of segregation in 207 cities and devised an index to measure residential segregation. Working on a scale from 0 (no segregation) to 100 (complete segregation), he found that half the cities scored a segregation index reading of 87 or more. The *least* segregated city scored 60.4.

White America, through housing segregation and the spider's web of zoning and occupancy laws, forces black Americans into the ghetto and then looks down on them for being slum dwellers.

Black America is overcrowded. The Census Bureau admits that "From 1950 to 1960 overcrowding increased for non-whites from 548,000 housing units to 633,000 . . . it declined for whites. . . ." Income doesn't matter. Nearly half the black families in Chicago making more than $7000 live in substandard houses, compared to only 6 per cent of whites in that income category. In Washington, D.C., a quarter of black families in the $10,000-and-up income bracket are overcrowded. The city of New York has officially labeled nearly half of Harlem's houses "slum." Nationally, almost a third of big-city housing occupied by Negro families is substandard, compared to less than a tenth of white-occupied houses. And that's just rosy when we look at the situation in smaller towns and rural areas, where 64 per cent of black housing is substandard, compared to only 14 per cent for whites.

And Black America pays more for its worse housing. The Chicago Urban League studied rents in that city and found that Negroes pay, on the average, $10 a month more than whites do for comparable apartments and $1500 more to buy comparable homes.

I served on the President's Commission on Urban Housing, which conducted an exhaustive survey of the nation's housing needs. Just a few of our findings include:

• Negro families, of whatever income level, pay one-third more for a given standard of housing than do whites.

• Eight out of ten Americans with an income of less than $2000 paid more than 35 per cent of their incomes for housing, while the majority of people with incomes of $10,000 and over paid less than 10 per cent.

• The proportion of black people in the central cities who can't afford decent housing will increase from 28 per cent in 1960 to 36 per cent in 1978.

• Discrimination keeps black families segregated in overcrowded ghettos although there are housing vacancies elsewhere. In Los Angeles, for example, we found that ghetto concentration increased at a time when the city's overall vacancy rate was 15 per cent.

There are more rats than there are people in Black America. The combination of inadequate facilities for storing garbage; old, rundown houses; and indifferent city sanitation collection and exterminating services result in a fast-growing rat population. When a bill to provide federal funds to assist cities in rat-extermination projects came to the floor of the 90th Congress, representatives of white America greeted it with a tasteless demonstration of bad jokes and puns. But rats aren't a joking matter; last year more than 15,000 cases of rat bites, mostly of children, were *reported*—the true total was probably several times that number.

Perhaps reformers take the wrong tack by arguing that rats harm children. The almighty dollar has more enthusiasts than do children, so white America may be more willing to respond to a report on the city by the U.S. Public Health Service that "the total economic loss due to rats in Cleveland is at least four million dollars per year."

Rats are more than costly nuisances or menaces to public health; they are symbols of the physical deterioration of the sections of our cities that serve as reservations for black people. In the ghetto, it is a major effort *simply to survive*. Well-off Americans, whose main housing problem is when to add that extra playroom or get that new kitchen equipment, find it hard to understand what it means to stay awake all night to make sure rats don't get into the baby's crib or to share a hallway bathroom with several other families. But the poor black families in bad ghetto housing have to live with these problems every day of the year; somehow they have to cope and survive. Somehow they must manage not to be crushed by their problems; and they must also keep their children from being crushed.

Black people have an unending faith in the value of education. Our history is replete with instances of whole families banding together to scrape up tuition to send one of their youngsters on to college. Nearly every Negro professional man I know was responsible for putting a brother, a sister, a niece or nephew through college after he started working himself. All too often there was no place for a black graduate to use his degree, and many wound up in the Post Office, but still the faith in education continued.

It was often dangerous for a black man to aspire to succeed in school. In many parts of the South, the Negro who planned to go to college was considered "uppity" and in need of a nonscholarly lesson from the Klan. The trees of many a Southern town were hung with the bodies of black men who dared to dream, dared to challenge a system that decreed that black people should live in perpetual ignorance.

And this is not ancient history. Black parents in most of the South today who dare enroll their children in previously all-white schools, or who exercise their "freedom of choice" options by sending their kids to such schools, have been cut off from credit at local stores, fired from their jobs, and hounded from their homes. Ghetto parents today are rising up against the educational establishment, which shows little concern about their children's failures and which is content with high Negro dropout (really push-out) rates.

Behind the call for community control of ghetto schools is the deep and abiding belief, in the face of all obstacles, that a decent education is the ticket to success. That belief may yet be fulfilled through educational reforms forced by a vocal, united black community and its white allies, but in the meantime too many ghetto children are doomed to failure.

The child who manages to survive slum housing conditions often cannot survive the miseducation he gets in ghetto schools. The longer he stays in school, the farther behind he falls in his studies. Black sixth-graders are more than two years behind normal achievement levels; by the time they are in the twelfth grade, they are more than three years behind. Schools with predominately black enrollment get fewer funds, older buildings, less-experienced teachers, and older books and equipment than do schools outside the ghetto. From the moment a black youngster enters his classroom he is aware of the all-pervading atmosphere of failure and inferiority.

And the chances are that he'll be in a classroom without any white classmates, for the "little red schoolhouse" is fast becoming the "little black schoolhouse" in our big cities. Washington's public school enrollment is more than 90 per cent black, and in cities such as New Orleans, St. Louis, Philadelphia, and Detroit, which have white population majorities, about two thirds of the students are Negro. Even in cities where there are few Negroes, school segregation remains, despite a fifteen-year-old Supreme Court ruling barring it. In seventy-five cities three out of four black children attend elementary schools that are 90 per cent or more Negro, and nine out of ten Negro students go to schools with black majorities. In the same cities, more than eight out of ten white students attend schools in which more than 90 per cent of their classmates were white.

The extent to which black children are damaged by the ghetto life and the inability of the schools to cope with educating them is illustrated by the frank testimony of Cleveland's Superintendent of Schools, Paul Briggs, before the Kerner Commission:

But what about the child of the ghetto? It is he whom we must save for we cannot afford to lose this generation of young Americans.

If this child of despair is a young adult, there is a better than 50 per cent chance that he is a high school dropout. He is not only unemployed, but unemployable, without a salable skill. Neither of his parents went beyond the eighth grade. Preschool or nursery school was out of the question when he was four, and when he was five he was placed on a kindergarten waiting list. . . . At six he entered school; but could only attend for half a day because of the big enrollment. . . . During his six years in elementary school, he attended four different schools because the family moved often, seeking more adequate housing for the six children. When he got to high school he wanted vocational training but none was available.

The family was on relief and he couldn't afford a good lunch at noon because Cleveland schools at that time were not participating in the federal hot-lunch program and the average cost of lunches amounted to 70 cents.

Of his few friends who were graduated from high school none had found jobs and they couldn't afford to go to college.

Here he is now, discouraged and without hope—economically incompetent at a time in life when, traditionally, young Americans have entered the economic mainstream as job holders.

A younger brother, age nine, is now in the fourth grade. He attends a new school, opened in 1964. Though he lives one mile from Lake Erie, he has never seen it. He has never taken a bus ride, except when his class at school went on a field trip. The family still does not subscribe to a daily newspaper. The television set is broken and there is no money to have it repaired. His mother has never taken him downtown shopping.

He has never been in the office of a dentist and has seen a physician only at the local clinic when he was injured playing in an abandoned house in the neighborhood.

At home there are no books. His toys, if any, are secondhand.

His shoes are too small and his sweat shirt, bought for 25 cents at a rummage sale, bears the insignia of a suburban school system.

Each morning he looks forward anxiously to the free milk he gets at school because there is no breakfast at home.

He can't study well at home because of the loud blare of rock-and-roll music from the bar up the street. There are nine bars in his rather compact neighborhood. . . .

The screaming police siren is a very familiar sound to him for he hears it regularly in his neighborhood, where the crime rate is Cleveland's highest.

These boys both have better than average intelligence but they are the victims of neglect and are lost in the maze of statistics. Their plight and that of thousands like them in America's ghettos can certainly be considered the most pressing unattended business on America's agenda.


Small wonder, then, that a study by the U.S. Office of Education—the most comprehensive study ever made of the nation's schools—found that the most critical factor in a child's school achievement is his sense of control over his environment. The child has to feel that effort is rewarded and that he can affect the things that happen around him.

The survey asked children to answer questions such as "Agree or disagree: Every time I try to get ahead someone or something stops me." And "Agree or disagree: Good luck is more important than hard work for success." The black youngster has before him not only his own impotence as reflected in his inability to get the bicycles or toys he sees other children playing with or sees on television, but also his parents' helplessness in a hostile world. His experience has been to see his father come home dejected after being laid off work, his mother crying because she has to keep him home from school because it is snowing out and she can't afford to buy him a winter jacket; his brother thrown into jail for the night because he objected to a policeman's calling him "nigger." Control over his environment is the last thing a child from the poor family in the ghetto feels; he knows he is at the mercy of outside forces in a way that a child from a secure, middle-class family does not. The emotional and environmental baggage a ghetto child brings to school crushes him, and the schools have not learned how to take the burden from his shoulders and help him to grow into the man he wants so desperately to become.

Children who come from families on the welfare roles especially lack the sense of control over their surroundings they need, for the whole welfare system is so structured as to encourage total dependency and to dehumanize the individuals receiving aid. The welfare poor are treated as if they are lawbreakers, and in a sense they are, for by their very destitution they violate the most hallowed values of an America that still worships the myths of self-reliance and individual initiative. To fail economically in this materialistic nation is to fail as a person and affront the more fortunate.

So strong is our historic aversion to welfare that only about a fourth of all poor people are actually receiving assistance. Stringent procedures to keep people off the rolls also reduce the ranks of recipients, and the police-state apparatus that ensnares applicants in weeks of investigations and harassment further reduces their numbers. Congress, in a moment of vindictiveness unparalleled in recent years, froze the number of children in the Aid to Dependent Children programs, which provides relief for children in families where there is no father present. It also empowered states and cities to force even those mothers with infants at home to go to work. The degradation of the welfare poor is matched by the degradation of the social workers, who are assigned to search their clients' closets and even to make midnight raids and snooping calls on neighbors to determine if a man is ever present in the house of ADC recipients. This so-called "man in the house" rule is responsible for the breakup of many families, since the jobless father is forced to choose between remaining with his family and letting them starve or deserting them so that they can qualify for payments that, despite the shame and abuse they bring, serve to keep body and soul together.

The payments are sometimes barely enough to do that. The state of Mississippi allots a mere $9.30 per month for each child, although federal funds would make up the bulk of any increase. Nearly all the states have relief-payment schedules that are well below their own standards of what is regarded as necessary for a family to meet the minimum standards of health and decency. In 1966, for example, the Ohio Department of Welfare set $224 per month as a minimum necessary for a mother and three children, but that same year state law limited the *maximum* payment to $170. A family of four in Texas is said to need $154, but the state pays $98; Alabama sets the standard at $177 but pays only $81. State welfare laws are a tangle of stupidity, vindictiveness, and insensitivity. South Carolina won't give aid to a blind person applying under Aid to the Blind regulations unless he lost his sight while in the state. Mississippi won't give aid to a mother and her children unless they have been without support for six months. And Louisiana's law provides that the mother of a second illegitimate child can be imprisoned for up to a year and fined $1000.

## BLACK AMERICA

Except for isolated experiments by some of the more advanced welfare departments in the country, little effort is made to restore people to self-sufficiency. In some states there is a 100 per cent tax on earnings of welfare families. Every dollar brought in from outside sources—even a child's shoeshining venture—is deducted from the welfare check, so there is no incentive for those able to work. A 1967 amendment to the welfare laws has softened this somewhat, but the basic situation remains: welfare regulations discourage people from finding full- or part-time jobs.

Most recipients—the overwhelming majority—can't work anyway. Of the 7.5 million persons who were receiving public assistance that used federal funds in 1967—90 per cent of the total of all welfare recipients—2.7 million were over sixty-five, blind, or otherwise handicapped; 3.6 million were minor children; and more than 1 million were the mothers of those children. A 1968 study by the Cuyahoga County Welfare Department (Cleveland) found that 96 per cent of its public-assistance recipients are unemployable— only 3 per cent were fathers who might become employable. Only 50,000 of New York's million welfare recipients are males considered employable.

Mothers on welfare *do want* to work. Seven out of ten welfare mothers in New York said they preferred to work rather than stay at home, *and 80 per cent of the Negro mothers in the survey said they wanted to work.* Part of the reason they can't work is the lack of day-care facilities for their children. Hiring baby-sitters for the day is out of the question since the salaries these mothers might command would be too low to absorb the expense. The Cleveland study found that 90 per cent of the mothers on welfare had at least one child under six years of age, and that the vast majority had no marketable skills.

But the public persists in believing the myth that the handicapped, the unskilled mothers, and the young children on the welfare rolls are "chiselers." In this they are aided by unscrupulous newspapers, which find that the best way to sell papers when little else is happening is to uncover a juicy case of "welfare fraud." Most of these charges turn out to be unfounded because, contrary to ill-informed public thinking, the honesty of welfare recipients is significantly higher than that of the general public.

The report of the Cuyahoga County Welfare Department declares: "If it were not sad, it would be amusing that every study made to determine the extent of fraud in public assistance has cost more to produce than the amount of fraud uncovered." In 1963 the U.S. Department of Health, Education and Welfare made an exhaustive investigation of families in the Aid to Dependent Children program in Ohio. Of the 37,000 families, they found only 5 per cent that were ineligible. Of the payments made in error, they found that only 28 per cent were overpayments and 42 per cent were *underpayments,* so that mistakes usually were in the state's favor. New York City conducted an experiment designed to see if the police and paper work involved in investigating welfare recipients was really necessary. Two districts servicing 22,000 families were instructed to take the applicant's word that he was in financial need. A check revealed that only 2 per cent filed false statements. As the Cleveland study says, "Indeed, comparisons of fraud among the poor with fraud by the general public in income tax reporting reveals the general public to be more open to suspicion and control than the poor."

Life on welfare—a life becoming increasingly common for society's leftovers in the black ghetto—is a life of hardship, hunger, and despair. White America, in the person of the welfare investigator, dictates and controls every aspect of the recipient's life. Two thirds of New York's welfare mothers reported feelings of "despair and resignation." Life is without hope, without dignity; and for the children, it is a life of overwhelming insecurity and dread. "Daily these youths have to face life," testified the Cuyahoga County welfare director to Congress, "with the realization that they have less of a chance to achieve a place in our society because they lack clothing, school books, and even shoes to attend school. Each night many thousands of children go to bed hungry, in housing that is inadequate, that is crawling with roaches, infested with rodents."

"Why aren't they motivated to better themselves?" asked a congressman. The answer serves as the answer of the black poor to similar questions harbored in the minds of the well-off: "The fact is that it takes so much strength just to barely exist that it would sap the strength of the strongest of us."

In the black ghetto everything is an effort, from fighting off rats to avoiding being cheated at the friendly neighborhood store. In fact, the real beneficiaries of the welfare system are the landlords, who are assured of high rents paid by the welfare department for rat-infested hovels, and the merchants, who mark up prices on the day welfare checks are mailed.

One of the grimmest problems faced by Black America is exploitation by ghetto merchants. In Detroit, an integrated group of 403 women took part in a massive comparison shopping survey of 543 food stores and 155 pharmacies in the ghetto and in the white suburbs. They found that ghetto-dwellers pay an average of 5 per cent more at chain food stores than do suburbanites. And in independent food stores —far more common in the ghetto—prices were 20 per cent more than at independent suburban food stores. Ghetto residents filling drug prescriptions *paid as much as three times what the suburbanite paid for the same product.*

The ghetto-dweller often pays his higher prices for inferior goods. Thawed-out frozen foods, spoiled meats, and damaged fruit are commonplaces in ghetto markets. Inferior hard goods—furniture and television sets—are sold for higher prices than are name-brand goods in downtown stores. And customers are lured into stores that advertise attractive prices for big-ticket items, only to be told they really aren't good buys; then they are deceived into buying more expensive goods. The profit in these transactions is in the high installment payments—often doubling the original cost of the item. Door-to-door salesmen frequently prey on the uneducated poor, misrepresenting the goods they sell, signing the unwary to long-term contracts with small print that binds the signer to extended payments he didn't know about. Often the small print binds the buyer to waive his rights if the contract is sold to a credit company. The contracts are often sold to finance companies that specialize in such shady operations. In almost all states, the victim has no legal recourse.

As Philip Schrag writes in the *New Republic,* "If Greedy

Merchant gets Ernest Black to sign such a contract for a new color television, and the set turns out to be an old, battered black and white instrument, or *even if Merchant never delivers any set at all,* Merchant can sell Black's contract to Ghetto Finance, Inc., for a lump sum, and Black is out of luck. Ghetto has a right to payment in full from Black, and Black has no right to tell a court that he's been robbed. Of course, after paying Ghetto, Black can sue Merchant, but first he has to find a lawyer willing to sue on a small claim, and then he has to find Merchant, which is likely, after the year or so that has passed since the sale took place, to be operating as a different corporate entity or in a different city."

This legalized robbery is executed with the full complicity of the law. The police power of the state and the full machinery of the law are brought to bear on the victims of such duplicity. Nonpayment brings garnishment of wages, an act that often means dismissal from the victim's job since few employers tolerate the paper work that goes with such payments. With all this awesome power ranged against him, the poor man in the black ghetto is forced to submit.

The battle to survive is not limited to the commonplaces of life such as shopping. Its major battleground is life itself. The health of the ghetto poor is precarious; Black America dies earlier and suffers from disease far more than does White America. One of the major causes of black unemployment is poor health.

In 1964, two Harlem areas containing a quarter of Manhattan's population accounted for 40 per cent of the borough's tuberculosis deaths and a third of its infant deaths.

Bedford-Stuyvesant, with only 9 per cent of Brooklyn's population, accounted for a quarter of its TB fatalities and 22 per cent of infant deaths.

Black Americans suffer disadvantages in health almost from the moment of conception. The death rate for black infants is triple that for whites, and the gap is still widening. "In 1950, the infant mortality rate for the non-white was 66 per cent higher than the rate for the white," declares one study, "but in 1964 the rate for the non-white was 90 per cent higher."

Forty years ago pregnant Negro mothers were twice as likely to die in childbirth as white women; by 1965 the gap grew to the point where black mothers were *four times* as likely to die in childbirth as white mothers.

Modern hospital methods have bypassed the black ghetto. Thirty years ago, fourteen times as many Negro mothers were delivered by midwives as white mothers. In recent years, the figure grew to *twenty-three times as many*. Tuberculosis is a disease commonly thought to have all but disappeared. Between 1960 and 1964, incidence of TB among white New Yorkers declined by 28 per cent, but for black people confined to the slums it actually increased. A twenty-five-year-old black American has a life expectancy of more than five years less than that of a white man. And the gap has grown since 1960!

Hunger stalks Black America. Americans aren't supposed to be hungry; hunger is something we read about that happens in India or parts of Africa. With storehouses bulging with surplus foods, no American can starve. That's the myth; the reality is in the hollow eyes of starving black children in the hell of Mississippi.

Doctors visited six counties in that state in 1968 and reported: "We saw children fed communally—that is, by neighbors who gave scraps of food to children whose own parents have nothing to give them. Not only are these children receiving no food from the government, they are also getting no medical attention whatsoever. They are out of sight and ignored. . . . They are suffering from hunger and disease and directly or indirectly they are dying from them —which is exactly what 'starvation' means."

To a large degree, the hunger that is the lot of rural blacks is the creation of local landowners and government officials who refuse to participate in federal food-stamp programs. Although the Agriculture Department had the authority to bypass recalcitrant local officials and distribute food in poverty areas, it went along with local bosses such as the Georgia sheriff who explained that his county turned down a proposed food program because: "It would just mean a lot of niggers lining up for food, and that's all there is to it."

That's not all there is to it—hunger has become a weapon to drive black people from the South. Now that farming has become mechanized, black stoop laborers are no longer needed. With no marketable skills, and with the newly won right to vote, the large black population of the rural South is at best a drain on the tax rolls, at worst a threat to the political power of the landowners. So the feudal lords of America's most primitive backwaters hope to drive their black residents to join the 3.5 million others in the past generation who pulled up stakes and headed for the slums of the North.

The emigrants know that life in the urban ghetto is hard, but they know it can't be as bad as what they leave. The black farm worker knows that jobs are scarce up North, but he also knows that work is scarce back home: the average black farm laborer works only seventy-seven days a year, earning a grand total of $353. These figures are for 1964, the last year for which such figures are available; the situation has not improved and has probably worsened since then.

What black Americans, North and South, share to a degree not experienced by white Americans is an all-pervasive sense of powerlessness. The black man is effectively excluded from a voice in any matters affecting him. To a degree experienced by few other minorities, the black man lives in an alien world that is frequently hostile to his progress and indifferent to his needs. He is powerless because he is unable to make and enforce decisions for his own community or to have significant influence in shaping the public and private institutions that control his life.

Chicago is a perfect example of the powerlessness of Black America. The Chicago Urban League undertook an exhaustive analysis of that city's decision-makers and found that black Chicagoans had virtually no part in the decision-making machinery that affects their lives. The League examined the racial composition of Chicago's leaders in the year 1965; conditions have changed little, if at all, and they can be duplicated in every city of the country.

Their report concluded that "... *it is safe to estimate that Negroes held less than one percent of the effective power in the Chicago metropolitan area.* Realistically, the power structure of Chicago is hardly less white than that of Mississippi." Some of the findings included:

- About 20 per cent of the population of Cook County

and 28 per cent of the population of Chicago was black, but of the 10,997 policy-making positions in major Cook County institutions, only 285, or 2.6 per cent, were occupied by Negroes.

• Only 58 out of 1088 policy-making positions in governmental bodies were held by Negroes. They were most evident in appointed bodies such as the Chicago Housing Authority and the Board of Education, but even there they held only 10 out of 77 positions.

• Only 2 out of 156 top posts in city administration were held by Negroes. Federal posts were also nearly all-white; only one out of 31 presidential appointments and 8 of the top 368 federal civil service posts in the city were held by Negroes.

• Private institutions have perhaps a greater role in people's lives, but a mere 227 out of a total of 9909 policy-making positions in the private sector were held by Negroes. The bulk of these were in labor unions and in religious and welfare organizations whose constituency is often the black community. In the welfare agencies, blacks occupied only 8 per cent of the major positions, nearly always at a secondary level.

• There were no Negroes in policy-making posts in the major nonfinancial corporations that dominated the city's economy and employment. Negroes occupied three tenths of 1 per cent of the policy posts in banks. With the exception of two Negro-owned insurance firms, there were no Negroes in important positions in the insurance industry.

• The city's big universities, which control expenditures of millions of dollars and which play a vitally important role in the community, including a dominant role in urban renewal programs, had only 5 Negroes in their 380 top policy-making jobs.

• Blacks were even frozen out of organized crime—only 5 Negroes were on the Chicago Crime Commission's 1967 list of 216 major and minor syndicate members, and only one of these was reputed to have even minor authority.

• Even in the sector where Negroes were best represented —labor unions—they were relatively powerless. Although blacks held 13 per cent of top union posts, only 2 to 5 Negroes were rated among the 100 most important unionists in Chicago.

• Black participation in the power machinery of Chicago, where it existed, came about by election of blacks by all-black voting districts or through appointments to public positions made in response to pressures from civil rights organizations.

Denying black citizens even the most elementary control over their lives results in more than economic and social handicaps; it causes psychological wounds that go far deeper and are far more disabling than any other form of hurt. The scars of oppression are seen in the faces of jobless men and in the deteriorating buildings of the ghetto, but the real damage is to the hearts and souls of black people, who must put up with a thousand daily hurts and indignities from a society that brands them inferior. The cry "Black Power" is the expression of the black man's frustration and anger at his powerlessness. It is a cry for recognition, a chant of desperation, an appeal for participation in his own destiny.

The black poor know that they are poor because they are black, and they know that, in a society that measures a man by the size of his paycheck, they don't stand very tall.

## BLACK AMERICA

Though they live in the midst of the most affluent society in the history of the world, they know they are the discards, the unwanted, the unknown. With powerlessness and poverty comes the realization that one is inadequate, unable to function, unable to protect one's family or to provide for them. The vindictive verdict of society condemns many in the black ghetto to lives of bleak, endless degradation.

Dr. Howard Thurman, former dean of the chapel at Boston University, describes the resulting alienation when he writes:

> To be ignored, to be passed over as of no account and of no meaning, is to be made into a faceless thing, not a man. It is better to be the complete victim of an anger unrestrained and a wrath which knows no bounds, to be torn asunder without mercy or battered to a pulp by angry violence, than to be passed over as if one were not. Here at least one is dealt with, encountered, vanquished, or overwhelmed—but not ignored.

Even blacks who have managed to escape the worst effects of racism feel alienated because of the experiences of their friends or relatives. The black child learns early—for his own protection—that white people can be dangerous, that they have power over black people, and that the child could be harmed if he angers them.

But these are feelings that human beings cannot live with for long. The self-imposition of controls to suppress one's anger and to accept the intolerable just leads to the buildup of tremendous inner emotions that can barely be contained. Because hostility and rage are turned inward, all sorts of deviations occur: illness such as severe headaches and stomach pains, alcoholism, drug addiction, gambling, street brawling, and a host of other self-destructive symptoms. As the anger gnaws at the individual, he suffers depression and anxiety, or seeks relief by withdrawal and apathy or by escaping into a drug- or liquor-induced fantasy world. It was no accident that drug addiction became a serious problem in Harlem only after the many fighting street gangs were broken up in the 1950s. With white society standing ready to punish assertiveness or aggressive behavior, the pent-up rage of the gang members had no release and they turned to drugs as an escape from the anxieties produced by their powerlessness and feelings of inferiority.

When a black nationalist in Cleveland, Fred Ahmed Evans, was arrested for allegedly leading an attack on policemen, the newspapers carried excerpts from an Army psychiatric examination made in 1955. The Army doctors wrote of Evans: "He is extremely polite and aloof. He is pedantic and guarded in his behavior. He is cooperative. This man has much hostility which he ordinarily controls but under stress it breaks forth with aggressive behavior. . . . It is believed that this man will probably have severe difficulty in the future in controlling his behavior."

There is little here that could not be said of millions of other Americans, but the doctors' report reveals some aspects of the black psyche that are peculiar to the black experience in which a black man who stepped out of line could face death or persecution. The doctors say Evans was "extremely polite" and "cooperative" as well as "aloof" and "guarded." We can see here the tremendous effort to suppress the true feelings. Generations of black people have been taught to treat white people with politeness and to be cooperative while hiding their real feelings behind a mask of aloofness, never letting their guard down for a minute. The tension caused by these contradictory requirements fuels a smoldering inner anger that "breaks forth with aggressive behavior."

Now, black people are freeing themselves from the need to suppress their feelings behind a mask of servility and smiling cooperativeness; the anger within them is being released. Doctors William H. Grier and Price M. Cobbs put it this way in their book *Black Rage:* "As a sapling bent low stores energy for a violent backswing, blacks bent double by oppression have stored energy which will be released in the form of rage—black rage, apocalyptic and final."

This is precisely the energy that is released in a riot. Riots are explosions of rage—the turning outward of the anger that has consumed black people for centuries, anger at being forced into rotting ghettos, anger at repressive police actions, anger at poverty and the multitude of humiliations that comes with being black in White America.

It is hard for white Americans to understand this. Even after the Kerner Report, many still clung to the belief that professional agitators, Communists, or "anarchists" were behind the rioting. But we were finally able to see the truth of the causes of the riots after the assassination of Dr. Martin Luther King, Jr., when most major cities were swept by explosions of rage and hurt. In city after city, the "it can't happen here" brand of thinking gave way to the harsh realities of race in America.

Many still can't comprehend what is going on. They point to the "slow but steady" progress, which they think will bring equality to black citizens in a generation, and they believe black people should patiently wait for the fulfillment of promises they've seen broken countless times. They point to the removal of the most brutal and overt forms of racism and expect black people to be thankful that lynch law is no longer commonplace. But the nineteenth-century French political philosopher De Tocqueville was a far shrewder observer of revolutions. "Revolutions are not brought about by a gradual decline from bad to worse," he wrote. "Nations that have endured patiently and almost unconsciously the most overwhelming oppression often burst into rebellion against the yoke the moment it begins to grow lighter. . . . Evils which are patiently endured when they seem inevitable become intolerable when once the idea of escape from them is suggested."

The yoke of oppression has been lifted just enough for long-suppressed feelings to come to the surface, but not yet enough for blacks and whites to work together for peaceful progress. I suppose that this period of violence has a degree of inevitability to it. The hurts and pains black people have endured for so long can't logically be expected simply to vanish. Doctors Grier and Cobbs write: "As grief lifts and the sufferer moves toward health, the hatred he had turned on himself is redirected toward his tormenters, and the fury of his attack on the one who causes him pain is in direct proportion to the depth of his grief. When the mourner lashes out in anger, it is a relief to those who love him, for they know he has now returned to health."

It would be far better for that health to come without the convulsions that have racked so many cities, killed nearly 150 people, and caused almost $1 billion in property damage and economic loss.

But mere release of anger doesn't necessarily change the

conditions that caused it. The individual rioter—and they were few in proportion to the over-all Negro population—may momentarily have vented his despair and frustrations. But when he woke the next morning to find that his parents' home had burned, that he couldn't buy milk for his kids because all the stores were wiped out or boarded up, he had to think twice about whether it was all worth it. The very enormity of the released anger resulted in an exhaustion that marked the return of the cycle of frustration. That's why so few cities have had more than one riot—the black community suffered such severe damage that it could not afford the luxury of yet another paroxysm of anger.

The important thing to remember about the riots is that they were not racial. They were not directed at white people as such. For every white person who was harmed, there were a dozen who were helped to safety by Negroes. The riots were directed at authority—at the visible symbols of white power in the black ghetto, and that included black policemen and black elected officials.

The targets in some riots were very selective indeed. Stores that had reputations for cheating black customers or refusing to employ black workers were hit while white-owned stores on either side of them were left standing. The symbols of abusive authority, such as the police in some cities, were prime targets. But white people were not attacked for being white, the way black people were attacked in other riots in our history—for example, Detroit's race riot in 1943, which saw black soldiers pulled from streetcars and beaten.

There was an element of a "return to health" in the riots in that the black community was momentarily united and found release from the destructive forces that tear people apart. But this release was temporary, and all of us in the civil rights movement know that the negative results of riots far outweighed the positive. I've met many people—most often young people—who disagree. They tell me that the savagery of the police and National Guard units awoke the community and brought home to the doubters the seriousness of the situation of black people. They claim that concessions were forced from City Hall, and that the spirit of brotherly cooperation has increased among black people.

To a degree this is true, but we lost far more than we won. Even the gains that have been claimed have been minimal: a few jobs in this city, a playground in that one. But far more jobs were lost as a result of white backlash in response to the riots. Congress reacted by cutting funds for job programs and tabling legislation that would have resulted in still more federally aided job programs. Liberal congressmen panicked at overwhelmingly hostile mail from their constituents and the spirit of reform quickly changed into one of fear and reprisals. Money cut from poverty spending was diverted into riot-control measures.

If riots helped to bring about a new feeling of militance in the black community, they also resulted in white militance of a particularly ugly kind. Vigilante groups sprang up, and frightened suburbanites armed themselves to the teeth, waiting for the black invasions that never came. The groundless hysteria that swept the country would be funny if it weren't so sad. Overnight, civil rights issues and economic issues became racial, and a polarized white society encouraged greater suppression and looked to police measures to settle social problems. The 1968 election campaign shows the depth of racial fears that gripped America. The main issue was not the disastrous war in Vietnam, nor was it the problem of how to end poverty. The main issue was "law and order," a thinly veiled code phrase for "keep the niggers in their place." In 1964 Alabama's racist governor George Wallace was considered a bad joke who pulled a few votes from extremists in the Democratic primaries. In 1968 he emerged as an important factor in the contest, with support among working-class and lower-middle-class whites in the North.

But we are a violent nation, and sometimes it takes violence to wake people up. The riots did have some positive results, although they must not be overestimated. The first is the shock value they had for millions of people who didn't realize the depth of black anger and the nightmare conditions in the ghetto. Businessmen, especially, responded with a maturity and hard-headedness that could be valuable in the long run. While some whites were forming vigilante groups, responsible business leaders were saying "We've been blind all these years. It may have taken fires and violence to make us see that we have a stake in the future of the cities, but now we do. And we intend to change."

Groups such as the Urban Coalition and various city committees were formed with the leadership of businessmen, and new jobs opened up. There were companies the Urban League had previously contacted—fruitlessly—to get them to hire Negroes. Now suddenly they called and asked us whether we could help them recruit workers. After Dr. King's death and the riots that followed it, my desk was overflowing with mail from people asking what they could do, and expressing shame and guilt. This kind of reaction is very encouraging. Today there are many more concerned individuals than ever before, and the shock of the riots had something to do with their newfound concern.

And we shouldn't underestimate the importance of the psychological emancipation that accompanied the outbursts of anger. Throwing a rock, to many, symbolizes the end of fear, the throwing off of psychological chains imposed by oppression. The release of that rage which, turned inward, has led to so much of the pathology of the black ghetto, can be seen as a healthy psychological phenomenon.

But the ultimate test of all action, including riots, is whether or not it produces significant changes. It is obvious that change has not occurred. Watts, four years after the first large-scale riots, is still an impoverished black ghetto. Detroit and Newark, scenes of the most destruction in the riot-filled summer of 1967, are basically unchanged. The shock of the riots and fear of their recurrence has led to greater sensitivity among officials in some cities; in others it has resulted in more vigorous suppression of the black community. The balance sheet shows some few gains, but the losses outnumber them.

If rioting is self-defeating, what then must black people do with the rage that accumulates under the hammer-blows of racism and deprivation? Well, there is another way out, and more and more black people are taking it.

Anger can be used in constructive ways. Aggression is sometimes released in violence, but it is also the fuel that drives men's creative impulses. It can be used to propel people into demanding their rights, knocking on doors of employment offices and schools, organizing their communities.

Real power comes not from shouting or burning down

one's own house, but from organizing group political strengths in order to control one's destiny. That's what other minority groups did. There were no shouts of "Irish Power" in Boston, but Irishmen quietly took over the city government and the poverty and oppression that afflicted the Irish in Boston vanished.

Black anger has to be channeled into the kind of constructive militancy that forces changes in white society. Black anger can drive a young man to excel over his classmates at school; to enter a profession and make his mark on it; to organize his community so that the heel of the oppressor is lifted. This is anger without violence, anger without vindictiveness. Aggressive energy can be a curse or a blessing, and it is up to the black community to transform the pain of four centuries into the instrument of change and equality.

I think we can do this because it is necessary for our survival, and black people have mastered the skills of survival. A lesser people would have died out a long time ago, unable to withstand the pressures of an immoral caste system. But black people, from time immemorial, have devised ways to survive. Some of these mechanisms, such as feigning politeness and joy as a cover for feelings of rage, took a great toll, but they were necessary. There were other survival techniques that worked as well, with less of a cost to the individual black man.

Black people sharpened the only weapon open to them —language—to develop a kind of wit and a whole vocabulary shared only with other blacks. Negroes used humor and their code language to confuse and frustrate whites without the open antagonism that would lead to sure destruction.

Black people even took the white man's own stereotypes

and turned them into positive virtues. Whites originally meant to stress a link between animals and Negroes when they came up with myths of the black man's physical and sexual prowess. But black people have simply said "That's right, I am better coordinated, have better rhythm, and I am faster and stronger than whites." Then they proceeded to create the music and the dances white people vainly try to imitate, and they took over the baseball and football fields that were once white preserves. Aggressive black men simply made the white man's myths come true, and they lined their pockets in the process.

Aggressive black men, kept from respectable professions by the color bar, turned their talents to other, related avenues. I've met some people in the numbers racket who could have been great mathematicians. It takes a great natural gift to keep that many numbers in your head and to make complicated computations without once turning to a pencil and paper. Today, they might win all sorts of scholarships and work on problems of higher science, but because they were black at a time when few young black men went to college, they used their gifts in other ways, no less important for self-survival for being illegal.

The skills of survival are present in the smallest child. I once met a teacher who told me that she couldn't understand how her colleagues could say that the children from the black slum the school served were uneducable. "I've visited the homes of these children," she said, "and I've seen the falling ceilings, dangerous streets, and the addicts in the hallways. I've seen the cramped space, with three kids sharing a single bed, and I know my students come to school hungry in the morning and nibble at a chocolate bar for lunch. The very fact that these kids have *survived* in that kind of atmosphere shows that they *can* learn." Any child who has managed to survive to the age of five in the hell of the urban ghetto has learned more about life than many whites learn in a lifetime, and he has proved himself a master at the most important skill he'll ever learn—the skill of surviving. These kids have developed a durability and a flexibility typical of black Americans.

We have heard so much about the pathology of the ghetto that we've been blinded to the real strengths that exist in Black America. Black people have been forced to develop psychological resources in place of the economic resources they've been denied. How else can we explain the actions of terrorized black tenant farmers in the rural South, who suddenly drop the happy-go-lucky mask they put on and risk their lives by registering to vote or sending their kids to a previously all-white school? Similar courage has been shown by black student groups demonstrating at the risk of expulsion, by welfare mothers protesting dehumanizing regulations, and by black parents demanding control over the schools their children go to. They all know the vast powers of officialdom and the risks they take, but courage and bravery instilled by years of practice of the techniques of survival enable them to take their stand. Black people today are utilizing the strengths they have accumulated in their struggle to challenge the system that oppresses them. The black ghetto is more than a tangle of pathology and social evils; it is the repository of skill and bravery that will help transform our racist society into something better for all people—black and white.

The central transmission belt for survival techniques and

the central bulwark of Black America has been that most maligned of institutions, that supposedly frail, weak, structure, the Negro family. Of all the distortions about Negro life in America, one of the most damaging has been the constant concern by white academic "experts," including some from broken families themselves, with the lack of stability of *the* Negro family.

For years scholars have delved into the historical and sociological aspects of Negro family life; few subjects have been so thoroughly studied. It was common knowledge that the Negro family, as a viable institution, dates back only to the end of legal slavery in 1863, and that Negro families suffer more disruption than white families, the result of various factors: the men are forced to migrate to the cities of the North, leaving their families; or, unemployed, they can't support their families; and men and women suffer the tremendous pressures and psychological damage brought about by racism. But in 1965, a Labor Department report, *The Negro Family,* was released. It purported to show that the instability of *the* Negro family was a prime source of the problems black citizens faced.

The intentions of the report's author, Daniel Moynihan, now a top White House advisor on urban affairs, were good. (The report was aimed at encouraging federal actions to strengthen family life.) Originally intended as an "in-house" paper for policy-makers (as usual, primarily white people), the report was leaked to the press and before long, thousands of column-inches in the nation's newspapers were taken up with discussions of what was wrong with *the* Negro family. Whatever its intentions, the report was used as an excuse for white liberals (and conservatives, too) to "cop out." If the reason for the gap between black and white achievement lay within the Negro community itself, in the form of family instability and illegitimacy, then there was no need for the massive programs in jobs and education that were being proposed. With the formidable backing any official document has, this "working paper" made many white people feel they had a right to point their fingers at the black community and say "Set your own house in order; you don't need any domestic Marshall Plan or other sweeping reforms." Such interpretations of this report shifted the focus of concern from the heritage of white racism, where it belongs, to the black community, which has enough problems without having to defend an institution that has been a historic source of strength and defense.

The saying that "you can't judge a book by its cover" is wrong when applied to this Report. Its very title offended: *The Negro Family*. It's not about *the* Negro family at all; it's about *some* Negro families, and a small minority at that. The implication of the title and of the substance of the report—that black families are going to hell on a roller-coaster—is factually wrong, too.

One out of four black families is headed by a woman, compared to only a tenth of white families. But that is not a valid comparison, since most white families are middle-class and a disproportionate number of black families are poor, and thus subject to the dislocations brought about by poverty. If white and black families of comparable incomes are compared, it will be seen that family stability is determined by income class, not by race.

( 59 )

A 1969 Census Department study indicates an alarming number of poor children live in broken homes, with the rate higher for black children because of the greater extent of ghetto poverty. But above the $4000 income level, the gap between the races closes, and the rate of family disorganization among black families making more than $8000 is virtually the same as for whites.

The black family has strengths which should be recognized. Considering the obstacles placed in its way by a hostile society and the persistent American attacks on black manhood, the stability of black families is extraordinary. The fact that the majority of all poor black families could manage to hold themselves together and meet every test of middle-class American standards for stability is nothing short of remarkable. *The* Negro family is not the one fourth that is broken, it is the three fourths that have held together under pressure that would devastate other groups.

*The* Negro family—the typical, average black family—is the 90 per cent that are self-supporting and the 50 per cent or so that have climbed into the middle class despite discrimination.

Illegitimacy is a problem, but again the figures do not tell the whole story. Illegitimacy is climbing for both blacks and whites—it is one of the few areas where the gap is closing. In 1960 the percentage of illegitimate births for blacks was ten times the percentage for whites, but by 1966 whites managed to close the gap to the point where the black lead was cut to six times the white percentage.

But no figures on illegitimacy can be trusted since so many cases go unrecorded. Out-of-wedlock births among white citizens are not fully reported because the vast majority are treated by private doctors rather than by public clinics and therefore do not become statistics. This and other factors are behind the U.S. Department of Health, Education and Welfare's caution that the figures ". . . probably result in proportionately greater understatement of illegitimacy in the white group than in the nonwhite. . . ." Abortions are another factor that renders the figures meaningless. In 1966 there were slightly more than 300,000 recorded out-of-wedlock births, but the estimated number of abortions was about one million—more than three times the number of births. Since costly abortions are beyond the economic means of most black women, it is estimated that whites accounted for over 95 per cent of the million abortions. When all these elements are taken into account, it is extremely unlikely that "immorality" among blacks is any more common than among whites, despite the fact that the majority of young black women come from poor families and often from a slum environment.

Efforts to slander black Americans by casting aspersions on their fictional immorality or family disorganization consistently run aground on the facts. Whatever problems exist are caused by the failure of white institutions to provide the economic, educational, and health services provided to white families. To shift the "blame" for these problems cannot obscure the resilience and strength shown by black people, and the fantastic successes they have wrought from a hostile environment.

The resurgence of black pride and the social and cultural renaissance taking place today are reflections of the internal strengths of Black America. Black people today increasingly feel that the energies once spent in futile attempts to emulate white people are now far better spent in developing the black community. This does not mean a retreat into separatism—except for some segments of the community. Our goal is full equality in an open society in which blacks and whites are equals, with the same choices open to all.

But continuing white hostility has forced new strategies required to create an open society. Black people today are placing more emphasis on the need for unity and on the desirability of creating a strong, stable black community capable of dealing with the white holders of power on a basis of equality.

To some extent this emphasis on black brotherhood is a retreat from the constant confrontations with a hostile society. James Weldon Johnson described the feeling as the ". . . desire for respite from the unremitting, grueling struggle; for a place in which refuge might be taken." The place of refuge is in the ghetto, in an identification with other blacks, and in a consciousness and pride of race that bear great similarity to the pride developed by other groups, a pride that enabled them too to achieve equality.

If White America reacts to this new black consciousness with fear, if it sees a threat in "natural" hairdos and African-influenced clothing designs, then these irrational fears merely indicate the deep guilt feelings that are the self-inflicted penalty of racism.

White Americans should welcome the resurgence of black identity and the fact that black people increasingly insist on the right to control their own destinies. It means that a dependent and repressed minority is asking to be allowed to stand on its own feet and to take its place in a healthy society.

# BLACK AMERICA

Black people want to do things for themselves. Even if it means failure in some instances, they want the right to fail. We don't want whites to do things *for* us, we want to do things *with* white people. This can be seen most clearly in the civil rights movement, where some groups unceremoniously told whites to get out of their organizations. This was a direct result of an "invasion" of summer civil rights programs in the South by bright white youngsters from the top Big Ten and Ivy League schools. They simply overwhelmed the black youngsters in the movement, who had had few of the advantages that let the white students excel in so many tasks. As the white kids took over the movement—"Let me do that, I can do it better"; "I'll write that piece, I'm an English major"—the black kids realized that here was yet another instance of white control and takeover. We in the Urban League never faced this problem because, as a professional organization, we have always had blacks working *with* whites in a peer relationship.

There are two main groups in the vanguard of black consciousness who will, I hope, provide the main thrust of the black community's self-awareness and its challenge to the evils of racism. They are the returning veterans of the war in Vietnam and the black students.

I visited Vietnam twice, and on both occasions I spent as much time as possible with the black soldiers there. Although blacks are only about a tenth of the population, they account for a fifth of the land troops in Vietnam, and a higher percentage of the casualities. Some of the front-line fighting units, including many of the elite troops, are 30, 40, and 50 per cent black.

Everywhere I met young men who were determined not to come back to the same situation they left. Many told me they joined the Army because they couldn't get jobs back home, and others told me grim stories of discrimination against their families in the States while they were bleeding under their country's flag ten thousand miles from home.

They shared a lot of the discontent with the war that all Americans feel, but they saw their participation in it as a license for equality. Their attitude was "My country told me to come here and fight; well, I'm doing that, but when I get home I'm going to be treated as an equal—or else."

They were getting a unique experience in equality at the front. Black sergeants were in command of white soldiers, and whites and blacks shared the same dugouts and outposts without any discussion about open occupancy. They were given an equal chance to die, and they were determined that when they returned to the States, they'd get an equal chance to live.

Out of my discussions with these young men came the Urban League's Veterans Affairs program. Staffed by veterans, this program helps veterans to find jobs, housing, educational facilities, and assists them with other problems. Our experience here confirms my first impressions in Vietnam: that these young men fully recognize that they performed as well as white soldiers in Vietnam, and now they intend to perform as well as whites at home. They want an equal chance, and they won't take "no" for an answer.

They are getting enough "no's" to indicate the depth of white racism. One young man sought a job in finance. A disbursing chief in the Army, he handled a monthly payroll of $250,000, but the only work he could find was a job weighing bags of coins and stacking them.

Another young man, a Navy radar specialist who studied

electronics at three service schools, said: "I went to several electronics plants back home and they tried to stick a broom in my hand."

Black veterans don't want brooms and they won't stand for the old saw "These things take time; be patient." One veteran said: "I don't want to hear any more crap about how much time these things take. It didn't take time to get my buddies killed in Vietnam, did it?" Well over 150,000 black veterans have returned home and more are on the way, and they share that attitude. They're bitter and they are angry —and they are skilled in the arts of war and the techniques of guerrilla fighting. It would be insanity for America to continue to treat them the way their fathers were treated. They won't stand for it.

More than any other group of blacks in our history, they have a sense of who they are and what they want from life. They possess the capacity for leadership and they have an ability and a sophistication that, if put to the service of the black community, as I believe they will be, could bring profound changes for the better in our society. The black veteran is not bluffing. He feels that he has looked into the face of death and walked away from it. He is going to challenge America peacefully, if he's permitted to, violently if he's not permitted to, and in ways far more sophisticated, far more destructive to the security in this country than anyone else has done. No amount of intimidation is going to stop him in his effort to be equal.

Black students possess many of the attributes of the veterans. As a group, they are more sophisticated and knowledgeable about what makes this society tick than any other group of young black people in our history, but they do have the skills and the impatience that are needed to effect change.

Like the veterans, they know they are the equals of any white person. They've overcome the disadvantages of poverty and bad slum schools to get into the top universities of the country. Once there, they saw the apathy and indifference of the supposed leaders of America's intellectual life to the conditions that surround them.

At first black students addressed themselves to changing the particular institutions they attended. They found admissions policies that opened the campus to few other blacks, bad treatment of the predominately black nonacademic staff, courses that rendered black contributions to America invisible, and they found the university exploiting blacks in the surrounding areas. They challenged all of this, often with a maturity not noticeable among white student reformers.

The spring 1968 student revolt at Columbia University offers an example of this. Initially, both white and black students took over the same office building, but it soon developed that the white students were more concerned about protesting Columbia's participation in the war effort. The black students explained that *their* major concern was with the gymnasium the university was planning to build in a city park adjoining the black ghetto, against the wishes of the people of the neighborhood. So they pulled out and took over another building, separating themselves from the main group. Their demonstration was in vivid contrast to those by other students. They conducted themselves with dignity and with discipline—no walls or furniture were defaced, no records destroyed. They presented their fellow students with an object lesson in how to conduct a nonviolent demonstration to protest injustices and still keep within the bounds of decent behavior.

Black students point to events such as the Columbia rising to explain why it may be necessary for blacks to separate themselves for a while to avoid being used by white reformers with a different set of priorities. The white students were concerned with ghetto conditions, but the real gut issues to them were the war and the draft. For black students, everything has to take a back seat until the ghetto gets its freedom.

Again, guilt-ridden whites often view black student solidarity with fear and alarm. They think there is something wrong with a Black Students Association on campus although they themselves probably belonged to the Hillel Society (Jewish student group), the Newman Club (Catholic students), the Dante Society (Italian students), or any number of other student groups in which those of similar backgrounds and interests join together.

When some black students on one northern campus asked to be allowed to live in the same building, the reaction was one of horror. "That's segregation; you can't do that," was the response. Of course, living quarters were rigidly segregated for years. Now that restrictions had been lifted, the administrators expected black students to scrape and bow and thank them for their liberalism. In effect, what the black students were saying was "I want to make my decisions for myself. You decided to keep us out for three hundred years, now you decide to let us in. When do *we* decide something?" Behind the black demands for separate living quarters were slights from white students, lingering discriminatory practices, and the simple desire to retreat from the pressures of the white world they were in all day, a world that remained hostile or, at best, wary.

They have already changed their colleges in many ways. Courses in black history are being given, black enrollment and faculty are increasing, and many administrators admit that the arguments of black students have brought these changes about. They are educating their educators.

Theirs is an impressive record, especially when you consider that this is the first generation of blacks to attend college in any significant numbers. Despite this, I am concerned about some trends among black students.

Too often I find greater concern with symbols than with substance. Too many young men and women think that if they wear their hair natural and sport *dashikis,* they are doing their bit. But a natural hairdo can cover up as much stupidity as a process; its what's inside your head that counts. Protest is important, but the way to beat the system that discriminates against black people is to achieve academic and professional success. Black students shouldn't be afraid of letting white students win the competition for who can shout loudest; they've got to concentrate their efforts on the competition for real power. Academically, politically, and economically, they've got to be on top if changes are to come.

The pitfalls are many. The tendency to seek self-imposed segregation is especially dangerous; it plays right into the hands of the bigots. Blacks, no less than whites, have to understand the need for diversity and recognize that security doesn't come from isolating oneself along racial lines. Separatism is just a way of copping out, and that's the last thing black people can afford to do today. Black students enjoy their opportunities because of the great sacrifices of others, and they have a responsibility to learn how to beat the system by making it work for them.

They have not yet, as a group, begun to challenge the institutions outside the university, although I expect that will come quickly. For this reason, the Urban League is working with black students to give them the skills and the know-how to effectively challenge the entrenched institutions that maintain the ghetto.

Up to now, the student's relationship to the ghetto has been more rhetorical than real; their verbal concern with the black masses hasn't been matched by their actions. Because we feel that black students have a responsibility to those in the ghetto whom society has left behind, the Urban League launched a new program in the summer of 1968, sending teams of students into the ghettos of America. They helped in community organization, research, helped black people to cope with landlords, welfare agencies, and city departments. They learned how to be effective, and we at the Urban League learned from them, too. As a direct consequence of this experience we placed three students on our board of trustees, where they have the chance to influence League policy and to deal with other trustees, who include some of the leading businessmen in the country, on an equal basis. I can't think of any other national organization that has recognized the needs of young people by placing nineteen- and twenty-year-old students on its board. This move is a symbol of our faith in the ability of young black students and our belief that their contributions are vital to the success of the fight for equality.

Black young people today, especially veterans and students, are fully aware of the uniqueness of the black experience in this country. The challenge to America is not to suppress or to stifle them, but to assure that conditions exist for their anger and energies to find expression in constructive ways. The future of both Americas depends on the chances these young people get to create decency out of the chaos that is the American racial wasteland.

Obviously, the growth of black consciousness and militancy means that the struggle for equality will be intensified. A great black man, often neglected by the schools because he didn't fit the mold of the "humble" black leader favored by our educators—Frederick Douglass—wrote: "If there is no struggle, there is no progress. Those who profess to favor freedom and yet deprecate agitation are men who want crops without plowing up the ground, they want rain without thunder and lightning. . . . Find out just what any people will quietly submit to and you have the exact measure of injustice and wrong which will be imposed upon them, and these will continue until they are resisted with either words or blows, or with both."

# CHAPTER TWO

# WHITE AMERICA

What white Americans have never fully understood—but what the Negro can never forget—is that white society is deeply implicated in the ghetto. White institutions created it, white institutions maintain it, and white society condones it. . . .

White racism is essentially responsible for the explosive mixture which has been accumulating in our cities since the end of World War II.

—REPORT OF THE NATIONAL ADVISORY COMMISSION ON CIVIL DISORDERS

THE AVERAGE white American simply cannot accept the accusation that he is racist. When the Kerner Commission blamed the riots on "white racism," a howl of protest went up from coast to coast. The truth always hurts, but in this case it hurt a bit more, because people don't fully understand what racism is.

Most whites were immediately angered because they interpreted *racism* as joining lynching parties, not wanting Negroes to sit beside them in a bus, or using racial slurs. But that's not racism, that is insanity. Modern racism is a good deal more subtle than that; it pervades our society and infects everyone in it.

*Racism is the assumption of superiority and the arrogance that goes with it.*

These attitudes need not be overt. A man doesn't have to go around bragging that he's superior because he is white, and he doesn't have to participate in brutalities against Negroes to be acting in a racist manner. He merely has to tolerate and condone the injustices that our society inflicts on the black man.

Throughout much of our history, white people who were racists controlled and dominated our country, and white people who weren't overt racists were accessories to the fact through their silence, and through their failure to oppose injustice.

White people who object to generalizations about racism are experiencing today what black people have been faced with for 350 years. All it took for a black man to be passed over for a job or for a home was to have a black face—all blacks suffered from white power and all suffered from generalizations universally shared by a racist society. Today, racism is so deeply embedded that even the legal and legislative victories of recent years haven't made much of a dent in it. Schools are more segregated than ever—fifteen years after the Supreme Court ruled that segregation was unconstitutional. Our public offices, businesses, unions, churches, and other institutions are almost as closed to black people as they ever were, and the voices raised against this racism are few and feeble.

We now see that laws are not enough. The test of racism today is whether White America is willing to give up some of its power and privilege and allow black people their rightful share of the responsibilities of power.

White racism created and controls the ghetto, and the silent white majority that condones this situation must accept the fact that complicity in such racism is evil. White individuals may not want our society to be split into two separate racial groupings, but when they sell their homes simply because a Negro family has moved into the neighborhood or switch their child into a private school because black kids are being bused into the public school, they are contributing to the ghettoization of black citizens.

Many white people who insist they are not racist still move into suburbs in response to the real estate man's whispered "We have a good class of people here"—the code language that tells them Negroes aren't allowed. They get exercised about "waste" in a poverty program while not saying a word about billions squandered in useless ways. They seize every chance to squirm out of their obligation to make ours a better society; their lives are a web of rationalizations and excuses not to become involved. And the net result is exactly the same as if they spewed out racial epithets regularly.

I recall once, after making a speech to a business group, a man came up to me and told me how much sympathy he had for "your people." "But I'm losing sympathy very quickly," he said. "The riots and violence are making me think I was wrong to support civil rights."

"That's too bad," I answered. "But while we had your sympathy, could you tell me what you did? How many Negroes did you hire? How many homes did your company build that were opened up to Negroes? How much support did you give to civil rights groups? Did you segregate your club or your children's school? I'd like to know what we lost when we lost your sympathy."

He could only stammer. "Well . . . I didn't do any of those things."

"Then we haven't lost anything," I said. "Nothing from nothing leaves nothing. But if you had done some of those things, and if all those other people like you who gave us 'sympathy' had done them, there would have been no riots and no violence."

I'm sure that man didn't think of himself as a racist, but he had the power to effect change, and he was silent. He helped to bring about the resulting frustrations that triggered the ghetto riots every bit as much as if he were an overt bigot.

And he exhibited another form of subtle racism, one he shares with millions of others. He presumed to judge whether a people should have their natural rights. I'm always hearing about how Negroes "have to earn their rights." Do white people have to earn *their* rights?

Black people suffer under a double standard, even among "liberals." I once took a trip to Eastern Europe with a select group of about twenty of the top industrialists in the country, men whose companies accounted for about 10 per cent of the Gross National Product. For many of these people, it was the first time they had had such close contact with a black man.

"You know," one fellow told me, "if all Negroes were like you, we wouldn't have a race problem."

"Do *you* know," I said, "if all *white people* were like me, there wouldn't be a race problem."

The arrogance of racism presumes that Negroes are somehow inferior, not quite like white people, and that only some few Negroes who pass the required tests of dress, education, and income might be included in the club because they are somehow different from those dirty, smelly people in the ghetto.

Black people have learned to spot racism where it exists with a radarlike accuracy that shocks whites who think they hide it well. Some of my own friends are shocked when I tell them that when they allow their three- and four-year-old kids to call their forty-year-old Negro maid by her first name they are teaching them racism. The only conclusion these young children can come to, since their parents' white friends are called Mr. and Mrs., is that blacks in inferior social positions, who are called by their first name, don't merit the same respect.

A black doctor I know is always being stopped by policemen who see a black man behind the wheel of a car with MD plates and assume it's stolen. Black professionals often find that when they walk into a luxury apartment building, the doorman looks them up and down as if Jack the Ripper were coming to violate every tenant in the place. A black businessman told me that once he placed a bid for a contract and when he went to the company's office to discuss the details of the job, jaws dropped and disbelief registered on the faces of the executives he had come to see. They just couldn't believe a black man was in a position to deal with them as equals. He is sure that he didn't get the contract because they didn't believe a black man could do a good job. Yet another friend of mine, who was thinking of buying a house in a particularly nice part of town, was told by a white friend who had known him well—they visited each other's homes often—that he would be "happier among your own kind."

Compared to the horrors faced daily by the poor who are imprisoned in the ghetto, these occurrences are minor nuisances, but they are part of the black experience in White America, random evidence of the racism that is part and parcel of our society.

Some white people feel that *thinking* racist thoughts is what makes racists. Because they don't think like a Southern sheriff, they believe they aren't racists. But their racism lies in the very fact that they *don't have to think about it*. It is so deeply ingrained that they simply assume a black man shouldn't live in a white neighborhood or that a black man can't handle a complex job. They *assume* whites are superior, and their behavior mirrors that assumption.

It is a perfectly natural conclusion for them to come to. People are the products of their society, and American society, from its inception, has been founded on the assumption that white people are superior. Black people were here before the *Mayflower* arrived, and within a very few years the colonists enslaved them. Africans were considered an inferior species of man, closely related to apes. Most of the "Founding Fathers" were slaveowners, including the man who wrote that "all men are created equal," Thomas Jefferson. Lincoln, the Great Emancipator, didn't believe Negroes were equal to white men and persistently tried to resettle blacks in Africa or South America. Legal slavery was followed by peonage and right up to the present day white children are taught racial superiority.

As Doctors Grier and Cobbs write, "The hatred of blacks has been so deeply bound up with being an American that it has been one of the first things new Americans learn and one of the last things old Americans forget."

Americans have created a stereotyped mythology about black people that invests blacks with all the projected taboos a repressed society is capable of imagining. Fantastic stories of the sexual prowess of blacks have taken root in the frustrated, overheated imaginations of some sick white people. Perhaps out of a sense of guilt over the persistent violations of black women by white males, they convinced themselves that black men have an insatiable sexual hunger for white women. Psychiatrists know that when people are beset by tensions related to their jobs or homes, their insecurities often come out in the sexual area. Thus many white men haunted by a sense of their own inadequacy often imagine that Negro men have superior sexual powers and are more desirable to white women.

Anyone who has lived in the South knows how strong

these symptoms of mental illness are in that region. They are common to people everywhere. The result of this sickness has been an overwhelming assault on the manhood of blacks. Black men suffered incredible restrictions that had their source in the twisted imagination of a repressed society.

At one time or another, forty states had laws forbidding marriage across racial lines, and it was not until 1967 that the Supreme Court ruled these laws unconstitutional. Such unions are viewed with horror by most white people, and some of the most open-minded whites I know will still say when they hear about an interracial marriage: "How awful, what about the poor children?" No one worries about the children when an Irish person and an Italian marry; few get so upset when a Jew marries a Christian. Why then so much concern when a Negro and a white freely decide they want to get married?

When you consider how rare interracial marriages actually are, you can see just how irrational such thinking is. To be blunt about it, most Negroes don't want to marry whites. Integration in schools, jobs, and other areas of life does *not* result in interracial marriages. Few people of whatever race marry the girl next door, or the girl they went to school with. People marry other people, not colors. Most interracial marriages are between people who are psychologically secure enough within themselves for race not to be a barrier. The resurgence of black pride, the "black is beautiful" feeling sweeping through Black America, should be assurance enough for those whites who need it that the goal of black people is not to marry whites. This has been at the top of the list of concerns of white people; it has been at the bottom of the list for black people. There has always been enough freedom, even in the most repressive areas, for men and women of both races to satisfy their curiosities and desires, and black people are too busy fighting their way to the homes, jobs, and schools they need to spend much energy trying to break down the most irrational of the white man's taboos.

The economic and psychological insecurity of White America is stronger today than ever before. In this mobile society it is common for people to move from low economic status to middle-class status within a relatively short period of time. During the Depression a quarter of the population was on relief at one point or another. Many of these people are now middle-class, their rise made possible by a host of federal programs—the GI Bill, home loan insurance, road-building, and economic and employment policies. The beneficiaries of these programs are often the most vocal opponents of measures to help today's poor.

The economic progress made by so many middle-class Americans far exceeds their educational and cultural advances, and so we are treated to an obscene display as high school dropouts, who make decent salaries as tradesmen or salesmen, scream about property values falling because a Negro lawyer or professor wants to buy a home in their neighborhood.

Many of these individuals who have just made it into respectability are hounded by the insecurities that accompanied their move. They are knee-deep in debt (financial observers are worried about the high rate of personal debt) and they are solely concerned with what they can buy and how to outdo their neighbors. The black man is a threat to such people. They've got to have someone beneath them or their status is valueless. Racism is their security blanket. If a black man can drive the same model car they do, if his children go to school with their kids, if, horror of horrors, he moves into their neighborhood, then he is as good as they are. They are no longer part of a dominant exclusive caste. The very foundations of their security are called into question. These almost paranoic feelings lead otherwise sane individuals to throw bricks through the windows of new Negro neighbors and to flee the cities to seek the security of all-white neighborhoods.

Some of the most insecure whites are those from ethnic groups that, until recently, met discrimination themselves. While White America has reserved most of its venom for blacks, there was still enough to go around to damage other people because they came from certain countries or kept certain traditions. It's hard to believe that as recently as 1960 there were questions raised about the loyalty an Irish Catholic President might owe the Pope. These attitudes are fading quickly, and some of the ethnic groups that remain in our cities are strongholds of antiblack feeling.

For many of these people, being a notch higher than black people is all they have in the world. As their neighbors and children move into the suburbs, they view the expanding ghetto with alarm and cling to a way of life that is changing. Black people want better homes and jobs, and this runs head-on into the desire of other groups to preserve their neighborhoods as ethnic enclaves and to guard their own jobs.

This conflict is tragic, for blacks and poor whites have both been left scrambling for crumbs from the table of an affluent society. Irish, Polish, and Italian workmen will benefit as much as blacks from massive programs to rebuild our cities and end poverty. Although a higher proportion of blacks is poor, most poor people are white, and the anti-poverty measures blacks are fighting so hard for will end white poverty too. And black workers aren't trying to get the jobs whites already hold; there is enough work to be done to keep everyone fully employed. Some jobs now almost exclusively held by whites, such as those in the building trades, are prey to slack seasons that wouldn't exist if our resources were applied to building all the homes and schools this country needs.

Clinging to racist attitudes for the sake of supposed status only delays real economic progress for poor and moderate-income whites, while it lowers the threshold of conflict in our cities.

Clearly, the relationship between blacks and members of other ethnic minorities is of major importance. Friction is bound to increase as blacks demand control of ghetto institutions and run into opposition from whites who presently run those institutions, often members of one or another of the ethnic minorities. When such confrontations have occurred they have been seen not as struggles between the powerless and the power-holders that accompany rapid social change, but as a black assault on a particular ethnic group.

This is behind the recurring charges of black anti-Semitism, resulting from the conflicts between the black community and white-dominated institutions such as the schools or businesses which, in some cities, are made up of people who happen to be Jewish. But Jews who are caught in such conflict aren't singled out because they are Jews, but because they are whites, whose presence in some ghetto institutions is resented.

In New York City, for example, many teachers are Jewish, and the bitterness between a black community intent on controlling its own schools and an educational establishment equally intent on preserving its privileges is unfortunately interpreted as conflict between Jews and Negroes. It is not. It's between concerned parents and educational bureaucrats. In Boston, where similar conflicts are just as heated, the educational establishment is Irish. In both cases, the black community is fighting to establish its own power and influence; the ethnic makeup of the present power-holders is incidental.

Another conflict area is business ownership in the ghetto. In many cities, Negroes moved into neighborhoods that were predominately Jewish. As these neighborhoods became black ghettos, Jewish storekeepers stayed on. Now many storekeepers are experiencing hostility. This is not anti-Semitism; it is a natural desire to replace whites who take profits out of the community. In many cities these businesses are owned by Italians or other ethnic groups, and the same friction is present.

It is important for both Jews and blacks to understand what is happening. In black communities the visible signs of white power are resented because this power has often frustrated legitimate Negro demands. Jewish teachers and Irish policemen are welcomed when they teach ghetto kids and patrol ghetto streets. They are resented when they don't teach well or when they abuse their power. Their religion and their nationality have nothing to do with it.

And their color shouldn't either. Black people sometimes exploit other blacks just as white people do. There are black teachers who crush their students' desire to learn, there are black storeowners who cheat their customers, and there are black cops who abuse their power. The overwhelming majority of blacks know this, and they welcome whites who want to work with the black community.

It is significant that when a Brooklyn school district controlled by an elected, black-dominated school board transferred over a hundred teachers last year, touching off a citywide teacher's strike and charges of anti-Semitism, they hired an additional 350 new teachers, half of whom were Jewish.

The Anti-Defamation League of the B'nai B'rith conducted a major study to find out just how much black anti-Semitism there really is. Their findings: there is significantly less anti-Semitism among blacks than there is among any other group of Americans. The reason for this is not too hard to understand. Black people are aware of the historic discrimination Jews have faced, and have identified both with the Biblical stories of the Jews in bondage and with the present-day persecutions of Jews—persecutions having more than superficial resemblance to the reign of terror against blacks in the Deep South.

Yet another factor is the unstinting support Jews have given black people in the fight for civil rights. Blacks recognize this and appreciate it, and they are aware of the fact that American bigotry lumps Jews and Negroes together as targets.

Unfortunately, some anti-Semitism does exist within the black community—we have our lunatic fringe too. And it has been played up by the media, which gives the most space to the most outlandish statements. A prime example of this irresponsibility took place on a late-evening talk show. Billing the program as a discussion of black anti-Semitism, three violently anti-Semitic blacks were gathered before the cameras and they harangued the audience for an hour. No other black viewpoint was represented, and the viewers of that program could only leave it with the false impression that blacks hate Jews.

The existence of a small but vocal minority of blacks whose anger at ghetto conditions and whose relative lack of sophistication lead them to make extreme statements has led to charges of "reverse racism." The undue attention paid to this minority seems another way of avoiding today's major problem—white racism. It is unbridled white power that created and maintains the ghetto, and white racism is behind the explosive frustrations in our cities.

Certainly, antiwhite feelings exist in the ghetto, but to label them "reverse racism" is to oversimplify the situation, to equate the bitterness of the victim with the evil that oppresses him. Black "reverse racism" is the response of angry people to their oppressors. It is based not on an existing caste system and the mythology that sustains it, but on very real grievances.

I certainly don't condone any kind of hatred, but I do think we should keep our sense of proportion and understand the violent emotions to which oppression gives rise. Perhaps the most relevant analogy here is the position some Jews take toward Germany. They know that the people of Germany today cannot be held responsible for the atrocities committed by another generation captivated by Nazi ideology. But many Jews still refuse to include Germany on a vacation tour or to buy goods made in Germany. They recognize that their attitude is irrational, but the memory of the murder of 6 million Jews cannot leave them. No one calls this "racism" or even "reverse racism." We realize that these are human feelings grounded in horrible experiences. So, too, antiwhite feelings on the part of some black people should be seen not as a kind of racism but as a response to generations of overwhelming oppression. White racism is a cause; black racism is effect.

During the period when Rap Brown was on page one almost daily, I spoke to many predominately white groups, and nearly all of them wanted me to condemn the things Brown was saying. Some people even told me that if I didn't blast Brown, Stokely Carmichael, and others, it would prove that I wasn't a "responsible leader."

I had to point out to these groups that Rap Brown didn't build the walls of the ghetto; he didn't keep black people out of pleasant suburban homes; he didn't bar them from decent jobs; he didn't turn ghetto schools into places where black kids are miseducated; and he didn't lynch any black people in the South. The concern with what Brown and a handful of others were saying was a diversion from the real battleground—white racism—which is the *cause* of extreme reactions.

White racism is the disease that is tearing America apart, and we have to study it and seek a cure for it, just as we do research on other diseases that kill, such as cancer. We won't be able to control the damage done by racism until we know more about why it exists and how it infects people.

We need to know why so many whites are psychologically dependent on identifying with a privileged caste system, even when they reap no economic benefits from it themselves. What makes people throw rocks at priests and nuns, as people in Chicago did during an open-housing march a few years ago? Why did the residents of Cicero, Illinois, deem an Al Capone a worthy neighbor, but refuse to allow any Negro to buy a home there, whatever his standing in society?

Perhaps sociologists will oblige us by dropping their preoccupation with the alleged pathologies of Black America and study the very real, corroding sickness of White America.

That something has to be done about racism is quite clear from the report of a special committee of the Joint Commission on Mental Health of Children, which wrote:

Racism is the number one public health problem facing America today. The conscious and unconscious attitudes of superiority which permit and demand that a majority oppress a minority are a clear and present danger to the mental health of all children and their parents. Traditionally, the criteria for defining public health problems are: (1) a problem that threatens a large number of people; (2) a problem that costs a large sum of money; (3) a problem that is impossible to treat on an individual and private basis; and (4) a problem that could cause chronic sustained disability.

This committee believes that the racist attitude of Americans which causes and perpetuates tension is patently a most compelling health hazard. Its destructive effects severely cripple the growth and development of millions of our citizens, young and old alike. Yearly, it directly and indirectly causes more fatalities, disabilities, and economic loss than any other single factor.

If we understand that racism exists less in overt acts of brutality than in the silent complicity that preserves the *status quo* that discriminates against black people, it becomes clear that the federal government and the Congress

**( 8 7 )**

are the institutions most responsible for the perpetuation of racism. I am fully aware of the laws that have been passed in recent years and the very real, determined effort of some recent administrations to break down the barriers of race and poverty. But the many responsible acts taken are more than balanced by the failure to mobilize this country's immense resources behind the kind of massive frontal assault that alone could overcome racism and poverty.

The various programs of recent years have been piecemeal efforts—mere Band-aids instead of the drastic surgery our sick nation needs. We hear a lot about how much money has been spent on poverty programs but, compared to other items in the budget, it doesn't amount to much at all. For those who believe we are actually waging "war" on poverty, it is instructive to compare the outlay for poverty programs with the war costs in Vietnam. Assuming these were in the vicinity of $24 billion in 1968 (that's the low end of estimates ranging through $32 billion), let's look at relative costs of some major programs.

The budget for the Office of Economic Opportunity, whose programs are generally lumped together as the War on Poverty, was $1.9 billion in fiscal 1969—*less than is spent in a month of the "other war."* The important Model Cities program, the basis of the effort to rebuild our cities, was budgeted at *less than a week's expenditures on Vietnam.* Manpower development training programs, vocational education aid, adult education programs, rent supplements, low-rent public housing, food-stamp programs to feed the hungry, school lunch programs—each was budgeted at a level costing *less than a few days of the war in Vietnam.*

Congress consistently votes programs into effect and *au-*

*thorizes* money for these programs, but that doesn't provide one cent. The money comes from separate appropriation bills, and these are cut mercilessly. Congressmen will often vote for a program so that they will look good to the voters back home, but when the money bill comes to the floor they turn around and approve cuts in the authorized amounts, rendering many programs meaningless. In the fiscal year 1968, for example, the rent-supplement program was authorized at $40 million—a small-enough amount. But the actual appropriation was for a measly $10 million—the cost of a few hours of the Vietnam war. Model Cities, adult education, and the Teachers Corps each got considerably less than half the amounts originally authorized—and that has been the story of most legislation. What this means to the ghetto can be seen by looking at the effect of cuts in summer job programs: in New York City, youngsters were cut back from 24,000 jobs to only 8400; in Chicago from 20,000 to 9000; and in Washington from 7000 to 2000.

It's misleading to blame the war for soaking up funds that might otherwise go to these important programs for there is no evidence that, if we had never gotten involved in Vietnam, the money would have been put to use at home. More likely it would have been returned to private individuals and corporations in the form of tax cuts, as was done in 1964.

Further evidence of this is Congress' free spending on other programs not related to race or to poverty. The space program, for example, got double the amount budgeted for the War on Poverty.

The net result has been to heighten frustrations in the ghetto. The announcement of bold new programs raises hopes that are dashed when allotted funds can't catch up to the glowing promises of federal press releases. The plain fact is that the division of the giant pie that is our economy has not changed much since World War II—some people still get enormous helpings while others get crumbs. In 1947, 20 per cent of people got nearly half the total income in the country. By 1962, they still got about the same percentage. In 1947, the bottom fifth of the population got only 5 per cent of the national income. *By 1962, even that disproportionately small amount actually declined to only 4.6 per cent.*

Many people are surprised at this, because they assume from all the publicity that social welfare programs are costly "frills" that are essentially "handouts" to the poor. The real handouts are those given to the rich, the middle class, and corporations. A wealthy individual can invest his personal fortune of $100 million in tax-exempt municipal bonds, get an income of $5 million a year from them, and never pay a penny in income tax. Middle-class suburbanites live where they do thanks to a road-building program that costs many billions of dollars and to costly federal insurance programs that guaranteed their mortgages. They can also deduct expenses for running their houses, while tenants in city apartments can't.

In the summer of 1968, while poverty programs were being cut to the bone, while a tax surcharge was being imposed, and while scandals of starvation among blacks in some Southern counties were dominating the news, *The New York Times'* Business and Finance section ran a large headline: SUBSIDY HUNTERS SWOOPING DOWN ON WASHINGTON. There were plenty of golden eggs for them to gather. The story stated: "It is estimated that direct Federal payments subsidies to private industry total $6 billion a year, and rarely show any indication of declining . . . subsidies payments are almost four times the Federal budget for the antipoverty programs administered by the Office of Economic Opportunity."

Payments to cotton planters alone totaled $935 million in 1967, more than half of OEO's budget. In a two-year period, cotton-growers got $1.8 billion in subsidies; they reinvested much of this in machinery that put thousands of black farm workers out of work, driving many into the swollen ghettos of the Northern cities to look for work, while their families were left to the tender mercies of Southern welfare departments. As investigators were disclosing malnutrition and hunger in the Mississippi county that includes Senator Eastland's plantation, the Senator was collecting well over $100,000 in federal cotton subsidies payments.

These subsidies are a form of guaranteed annual income for farm operators, since they insure them a minimum income, something that made sense when most farms were family-run enterprises, but which seems strange in these days of agricultural factories run by large corporations. One such agricultural corporation in California got $4 million in subsidies. Among those "farmers" who got federal farm payments was the Louisiana State Penitentiary, which got $89,697.

Total subsidies for agriculture are $4 billion a year. They go to tobacco-growers, peanut-growers, and they help sugar-growers maintain prices at three times the level of world sugar prices, which results in higher prices for ghetto housewives. Others feed at the federal trough, too. "It is estimated," *The Times* reports, "that commercial aviation receives directly or indirectly about $750 million of the Federal Aviation Administration's budget of $800 million a year." Even these expenditures pale beside the government's multibillion dollar backing of the supersonic airplane. Shipping lines get $200 million a year in direct payments, and private shipbuilders get more than half of that.

Indirect benefits abound as well. Research grants to private corporations are common. Whole industries do most of their business with the government. If indirect subsidies such as the oil depletion allowance, tariff protection laws, and similar government aid to industry were lumped with direct subsidies, the total would come to nearly $9 billion a year.

I am not proposing that we do away with all of these programs of federal aid to individuals and corporations, although many couldn't possibly be justified. I'm just asking that this generosity be extended to those who need it most —America's nearly 30 million poor people.

The limited scale of aid provided now prevents many of our urban problems from being solved. Last year the Urban League compiled a study of 815 federally financed antipoverty programs in 79 cities—more than three quarters of them showed good-to-excellent results. But the poverty program has reached only one tenth of out-of-work, out-of-school youngsters, and retraining programs have reached only one tenth of the 2 million workers who need them most.

A dollar shortage also defeats the intent of the civil rights laws. It is one thing for government to tell employers that discrimination is illegal, but unless the law is rigidly enforced —and that means well-staffed inspection and compliance offices—it is meaningless. The Equal Employment Opportunity Commission, which deals with complaints of discrimination in employment, has a fifteen-month backlog of more than 2000 cases, because its staff is too small and Congress cut its funds. The EEOC warned Congress that, because it can't move swiftly, it may be "contributing to the current unrest" by frustrating those who file complaints and get no action. Integrated schools and open housing are the law of the land, but the machinery to enforce them is either feeble or nonexistent.

There simply has not been the kind of commitment to the cause of equal rights that would make a difference in the present crisis. The problems of racism and of poverty have not had the priority and the massive support that would make their solution possible. When the steel companies announced price hikes, they came under tremendous pressure —federal officials publicly accused them of endangering the nation's economic stability, and federal contracts were withdrawn to force them to retreat. How many plants can you name that lost defense contracts because of discriminatory practices? How many federal officials do you know who were fired for discriminatory hiring within their departments? None. Yet such discrimination exists, and it is against the law.

The federal government is the largest employer in the country, and it should be setting standards in fair employment practices for private industry. It isn't. Only a third of black government workers have white-collar jobs, compared to over half of white employees. Between 1962 and 1966, more than 40,000 persons got jobs in the higher-paying GS12-18 categories; only 4 per cent were black. In 1966, 41.7 per cent of the employees of the Government Printing Office were black, but there wasn't a single black man in the higher-paying jobs that carried more responsibility. Agencies such as the Department of Health, Education and Welfare or the Department of Housing and Urban Development, which deal with the problems of the cities and with the black poor, filled only about 3 per cent of top posts with black people. Uncle Sam, despite all the talk of equality, still reserves his brooms for black people.

The message of recent years is that good intentions aren't enough. Certainly the Johnson administration was concerned with rebuilding our shattered domestic peace and reclaiming the nation from its heritage of racism—and it produced more concrete gains for black people than any other administration in history. But it is a measure of the enormity of the problem that even the measures taken were too little and too late. The Congress passed a few civil rights laws that lacked adequate enforcement provisions and didn't touch most people's daily lives at all, and it passed a number of imaginative though underfunded programs. Then it sat back and congratulated itself on its accomplishments while the black ghetto continued to suffer economic deprivation. The very real problems dividing the country were never given the funds, the priority, or the timetable for solution that other, far less important programs got.

Partly these failures can be blamed on the weaknesses of Congress as an institution. We have a horse-and-buggy Congress in the space age. The dead weight of the seniority system has concentrated power in the hands of the most reactionary elements. Safe one-party districts, in the South or in boss-ridden areas elsewhere, return the same men to Washington year after year. Their seniority gives them positions of leadership and all-important committee chairmanships, leaving them well-placed to squash progressive legislation. The stranglehold these examples of Neanderthal sensitivity have on the future of this country has to be broken if Congress is to become an instrument of change. It may be true that the bigotry of some congressmen merely reflects the thinking of their constituents, but the price we all pay for placing such people in positions of authority beyond that to which they have been elected is awesome.

A part of the blame for the failure of the Congress and of the government must be placed at the door of the liberals who have run the federal establishment for most of the past generation. Liberal congressmen have often lost important legislation or seen it weakened because they didn't work as hard as their opponents, or because they didn't have the kind of legislative savvy that comes as second nature to many reactionary congressmen from the South. I must admit to a grudging admiration for the skills of Senators such as Richard Russell of Georgia or Sam Ervin of North Carolina. Their intimate knowledge of the rules of the Senate and their hard work and doggedness have managed to defeat or weaken important pieces of legislation. There have been few liberal lawmakers who could match their skill—Hubert Humphrey in his Senate days was one—and the lack has harmed the country.

But the failure of liberalism goes deeper. Historically, the liberal has been a talker rather than a doer, a describer of injustice who could rally public opinion rather than a decision-maker who used his power to end injustice. The liberalism of many people increases with the distance of the problem. When the racial problem was seen as one of Southern lynchings or separate drinking fountains, liberals were loud and aggressive in their denunciations. But their liberalism is muted now that the problem has moved north and the issues are closer to home.

It is much easier to urge federal control than it is to assume responsibilities at the local level. Many of the intellectuals who profess a liberal philosophy don't want to get their hands dirty by doing the hard work required in their own communities. They don't want to ring the doorbells and get into the rough and tumble of politics, to go out and convince their neighbors that social evils have to be eliminated. They'd rather talk to each other and deal with abstract issues.

What liberals will have to understand if they are to be effective in bringing about an Open Society is that they have to get their hands dirty once in a while. They'll have to learn to play the game—and by that I mean sitting down with conservatives in Congress and dealing with them on a political level. If it means trading a few post offices to get a ghetto job program through Congress, they've got to be ready and able to horse-trade. The liberal who supports a housing bill calling for construction of a million housing units has to make a choice. He can support the bill all the way—and watch it lose. Or he can accept a compromise that calls for 700,000 units. All too often the liberal prefers defeat to compromise. He'll retreat to his ten-room house in a neat suburb and boast of his unsullied principles; but 700,000 people will go homeless because he doesn't understand the difference between principles and tactics. The real principle is getting a housing bill through; the number of units is tactical. Apparently the Southern conservative, who would never confuse his ultimate aims with the tactics required to achieve them, cares more about maintaining the *status quo* than the liberal cares about changing it.

There is an arrogance in the liberal's attachment to ideals unsullied by the give and take of politics—an "I know best" quality that assumes superior knowledge of the needs of the people he is presumably concerned with. This streak of paternalism has always been prominent among the friends of the black man. The early abolitionists had it, and this missionary "white man's burden" attitude continues to the present day, especially in institutions such as welfare departments and the schools, which are often staffed by liberals. A supplementary report to the Kerner Commission analyzed welfare workers and concluded:

"There is an element of paternalism in their views of their clients: they believe their mission is to teach middle class ways as much as to help their clients help themselves. Other groups in the city see social workers as leaders in the struggle for equal rights for Negroes, but the social work rank and file is not particularly active."

I think we can say that the paternalistic, ineffective liberal is the "black man's burden." One of the reasons the anti-poverty program ran into trouble was that liberals in the federal government and local administrations mistrusted the poor. The provisions for "maximum feasible participation of the poor" struck terror into the hearts of liberal "experts" who see all new federal programs as something that they alone can run. But the black poor know that good intentions don't always bring good results and that they had been brutalized and their neighborhoods demolished by other liberal administrators. The black poor insisted on running these programs themselves, and the resulting conflict brought liberals and conservatives together in their mistrust of the poverty programs that dared to let black people exercise power. It was the same liberal arrogance that led to the creation of new structures to administer these programs, when the money could have been funneled through subcontracts to organizations such as civil rights groups and church and community groups in which black people already had dominant roles. The failure to recognize that Black America wanted control at least as much as it wanted the programs themselves led the antipoverty program up some rocky paths.

Another failing of some liberals is lack of stick-to-it-iveness. When the going gets hot, they find themselves another issue. After the Meredith March in Mississippi in 1966, when the first raucous cries of "Black Power" were heard, liberals outdid each other in trying to get off the civil rights bandwagon and into the antiwar movement. Vietnam was actually a safe haven for many who realized that the time for the "great white father knows best" type of liberal was ended and that, from here on in, whites in the movement would have to work a lot harder—and with other white people at that. Somehow many conservatives found the energy to be both for the war and against civil rights, but some liberals became totally preoccupied with the Vietnam issue and put civil rights on a lower level of priorities. This fickleness of some of our liberal allies has damaged the cause of black Americans. We need full-time allies, for creating an Open Society is a full-time task.

Black people haven't got the options available to the part-time liberals. Black people couldn't say, as some liberals did in the 1968 election, "I refuse to vote for the lesser of two evils, I'm going to sit this election out." Black people knew that the next four years would be life-and-death years for millions of black kids in the schools or entering the work force. They knew that they couldn't afford the luxury of not voting for the most liberal candidate in the running. The white liberal could say he would spend the next four years "reorganizing the Democratic Party," but the black man knows that change doesn't come about through dreaming of a non-existent political purity.

The arrogance some liberals exhibit is mitigated by their very real past accomplishments. Some of the more vocal radicals can't even point to past services to black people, although they pretend to speak for blacks in their efforts to change society so that it conforms to what *they* think it ought to be. These are the people who have opted out of our society "because it is so evil." Again, they can do so because they have the options. Black people have only two options—to suffer in the ghetto or to work within the system to change it.

The New Left, the disillusioned liberals, the new radicals —all express a distaste for the present system that is shared in large measure by black people. But blacks can't afford to indulge in the fantasies of romantic coffee-house revolutionaries who compensate for their impotence by wild talk. Black people comprise only a little more than a tenth of the population, have perhaps 2 per cent of the wealth and no major weapons at their command; they cannot hope to overthrow the system by violent means. To attempt it is to court self-destruction and genocidal reprisals. By organizing the black community to put intense pressures on society, we can create a social revolution that brings equality for black people. This is somewhat less than the apocalyptic daydreams of frustrated radicals, but a result more in line with what black people really want.

We are once more up against the arrogance of some white people who presume to know what is best for blacks. While the white radical is full of fine-sounding statements about the dehumanization of work patterns in America and is contemptuous of jobs such as assembly-line work in a factory, the black worker desperately wants those very jobs so that he can feed his family. While a black man might agree that there are elements of our present system that are thoroughly evil, he realizes that in order to change them he must first take his place within the system. You can't opt out of anything you aren't part of, and you can't effectively work to change it from the outside, either.

I recall a recent lecture I gave at a Negro college in the South. During the discussion period I was challenged by some young white faculty members who held that teaching math, physics, and other subjects was a waste of time. What their students really needed, they said, was instruction in revolution and in changing the system. They wanted to use black students to achieve their own ends. Their students *can* change our institutions—by first getting jobs within the major corporate structures in the country, and then using their influence and power to make them responsive to the needs of black people. But I know of no corporation that is looking for a graduate with a degree in revolution. Those young white radicals who were so arrogantly sure of what was best for their students took care to get their own degrees first. And they didn't storm the barricades in the financial centers of the North; they sneaked down South to a little black college where they could play the great white father role by telling blacks what was good for them. If they succeed in provoking the revolution they are prattling about, and if it fails, they can simply say "Sorry about that," and go back into the system—having taken care to equip themselves with the necessary degrees and qualifications. To play on the very real grievances and justified anger of black youngsters in order to promote their own ideological beliefs is not only dishonest, it is cowardly. They are asking black people to take the risks while they do the theorizing. I see little difference between this attitude and the more overtly destructive racism of the society they claim to want to change.

When you examine the radicals who are egging blacks on, almost without exception they are people who are well off, hold good jobs, and enjoy the fruits of the white society that is closed to blacks. I once was on a television panel show with a well-known author who spent the whole program talking about how bad the educational system was and how we ought to do away with schools altogether. Money, he said, is unimportant; it doesn't bring happiness and it doesn't insure morality.

I had to suggest to him that he go into the ghetto tenements and tell people there that money was an unnecessary evil and that they should be happy in their poverty. He could say all those cute things because he was financially secure; he could run down the value of education because he had a college degree. Black people who are poor can't afford the intellectual extravagance of such empty theorizing. Education and money are what they need most—they know what life is like without them.

Some radicals feel they have to outdo the most extreme statement by militant blacks in order to keep their radical credentials. So we have white professors and clerics who live in lily-white suburbs writing profusely about how Negroes ought to be happy living in the ghetto and about how our strategy should aim for separation from evil whites. The smugness of their pronouncements hides the fact that they have nothing to lose if these things come to pass; and it hides an underlying racism too.

Racism is not just doing evil to a black man, it's also putting up with outrageous behavior from him simply because he is black. The condescension implied is as racist as that of any bigot who says "Well, Negroes don't know any better." Early in 1968 the New Left held a convention in Chicago, and a small group of blacks in attendance—perhaps 10 per cent of the total number of delegates—organized themselves into a black caucus. The white radicals fell all over themselves trying to comply with the ridiculous demands of the blacks. They gave them half the votes in the convention, approved insulting resolutions, and listened to wild talk that debased the purpose for which they assembled. In doing this they exhibited a subtle kind of racism themselves, for their implicit assumption was that the blacks had to be humored and pacified; that no outrage was too great not to be accepted from the poor, oppressed blacks.

I call this the "hit-me-again" syndrome, and I've seen it countless times. There are some white people who use guilt over the injustice done to blacks to resolve their own personal conflicts. They like nothing better than to listen to a black man curse them out and threaten them. I don't happen to think that the mission of black people in America is to play this kind of game with people who are themselves in need of assistance and who exhibit, in the process, a racism no less real for being twisted into an unusual form. A radicalism centered about vague revolutionary impulses, without program and without purpose, is the kind of radicalism that is self-defeating.

America has a unique skill: It is flexible enough to change in proportion to the concrete demands made by groups that bring strong pressure to bear. The "system" changes, not because of a handful of pseudo-revolutionaries but because major segments of the population organize around issues that concern them deeply and apply pressures that are ultimately intolerable to the system. The prime example of this in our times has been the rise of unionism.

At one time unions were considered to be great evils. A union organizer, like a civil rights worker, was viewed as a dangerous radical, and was subjected to beatings and even murder. In the great wave of industrial unionism in the early 1930s, strikes were marked by violence and police action. Workers sat-in at plants and fought off goon squads hired by employers. Labor's disruptive tactics forced the system to accommodate its demands: unions were recognized and protected by federal law, workers won salary increases and took their place among the stable elements of the society that once fought them tooth and nail.

The resemblances to the civil rights movement are obvious. Today people talk about the way Negroes take their demands into the streets and disrupt normal processes as if it were some kind of new and dangerous tactic. It's not. The labor movement used the same tactics to make this country more humane and more responsive to the demands of the outcastes of an industrial society.

Labor was the moving force behind such legislation as Medicare, Social Security, minimum wage laws and workman's compensation laws, and the power of many unions helped the civil rights movement register its gains in the early 1960s. Union membership has meant the difference between comfort and poverty for many a black man, and black people have always maintained close ties with the trade union movement. Whatever our current differences with some segments of the labor movement today, black people aren't about to forget the great historic role it has played in the past.

The fact that labor led the way in bringing about the social reforms of the past probably accounts for the great disillusionment with many unions today. A few unions have regressed to the point where their members are among the strongest bulwarks of white supremacy in American life.

Even the strongest friends of labor, and I consider myself one who has always been a strong supporter of unionism, must reluctantly admit that as a whole the labor movement seems to have lost its passion for justice, and seems content to confine itself more to narrow economic gains for its members. Labor today, to many, presents an image of a protective association, filled with middle-class people who have advanced rather quickly and are preoccupied with maintaining the *status quo* and are increasingly hostile to efforts of minority groups to join them in their newfound prosperity.

Labor has failed to use its skills to organize the great numbers of workers in marginal industries whose paychecks, after a grueling week's work, are less than the poverty standards. In large measure, it has turned its back on the poor, the black, and the helpless. When Cesar Chavez organized a strike of California farm laborers, primarily Mexican-Americans, organized labor was indifferent to his pleas for help until Walter Reuther's auto union helped foot the bill. After that, helping Chavez became respectable and other unions demonstrated their support. But millions of other farm workers and urban workers remain unorganized and labor leaders seem more interested in discussing the investment of their giant pension funds than in bringing the benefits of unionism to the poor and the hungry.

Some of the unions historically most intent on freezing black workers out of higher-paying jobs are those in the building trades and the skilled crafts. Many of these unions have apprenticeship programs leading to full journeyman status. Despite the efforts of the civil rights organizations, the Labor Department, the Justice Department, the courts, and the leadership of the AFL–CIO itself, these are still largely racially unrepresentative. The Equal Employment Opportunity Commission examined the racial makeup of trainees in carpentry, plumbing and pipefitting, and electrical work in three big states—California, New York, and Michigan. Out of 23,497 apprentices only 951, or 4 per cent, were Negroes. In 1968, less than 1 per cent of the 1449 plumber-pipefitter trainees in California were black.

Lately there have been signs that some of this union resistance is being overcome. Black building trades apprentices doubled in the first half of 1968—half of the new recruits coming from a joint union-Urban League program.

Public statements from some union leaders also indicate that change is on the way in this hard-core area of resistance.

But it still sometimes takes a federal court order to get a qualified black applicant into a union. Local 212 of the International Brotherhood of Electrical Workers succeeded in keeping a black electrician (who had a college degree and had passed a journeyman's test in another state) out of the union for ten years, until a federal court in Cincinnati ordered him accepted.

In a now-famous 1966 case, a local of the Sheet Metal Workers in New York was ordered by a court to give impartial tests to new applicants to the all-white union. Negro and Puerto Rican applicants got intensive coaching from the Workers Defense League and passed the test with flying colors—nine of them placed among the top ten. But instead of praising the young men for their hard work and determination, the union yelled "foul" and insisted that they must have had the answers beforehand.

A 1955 promise of the then newly merged AFL–CIO said that it would eliminate racial discrimination among member unions, yet while some unions have been expelled for corruption, not a single union has been expelled from the organization for racial discrimination.

Some union racism is subtle. Although it wasn't until 1966 that the 40,000-member Brotherhood of Locomotive Engineers dropped an all-white provision in its constitution, overt bias is rarely so blatant. Sometimes it takes the form of negotiating seniority systems that place blacks in menial jobs, evading federal laws by accepting a few token members, and using hiring halls and referral systems to keep blacks from bidding for jobs. The NAACP has filed over seven hundred complaints of union discrimination with agencies of the federal government.

When all else fails, some unions take refuge in tests that work against blacks with inadequate ghetto educations. "Czolgosz is to Booth as McKinley is to (a) Lincoln, (b) Washington, (c) Roosevelt, (d) Garfield" is one such question on a test given applicants to a building trades union.

It is unfortunate that the disgraceful behavior of some unions makes the whole movement look bad. Quite a few unions have compiled excellent records in recent years; they recruit black workers, fight for civil rights, and carry out social projects of great importance, often in the face of opposition from bigoted members. Many white auto workers voted for Wallace in 1968, but that didn't stop Walter Reuther from actively fighting for equal rights. The UAW, in fact, is one of the few unions that has taken action against locals for racial discrimination. So too have the Packinghouse Workers. Such locals as New York City's Local 1199 of the Hospital Workers and District 65 of the Distributive Workers are among many outstanding examples of labor's continuing role in fighting for the rights of the poor.

Some union leaders would like to be more progressive but are afraid they'll be voted out of office by a membership that is out of sympathy with any moves toward equality. Ironically, some of this growing unionist conservatism is a direct result of the success unions have had in raising the standard of living of American working men.

Half of all union members make over $7500 a year, and half live in the suburbs where, as first-generation homeowners, they are more worried about taxes and Negroes moving into their neighborhoods than they are about social justice.

Their irrational fears are misdirected, for their gains are not yet so secure that they can turn their backs on progressive union policies. The labor rank and file must come to understand that its future is only secure to the extent that it lives up to its pledge to fight for the rights of all working people. There is still plenty of antilabor feeling in the country, and union men can't afford to turn their backs on the natural allies they have in black people and young whites. Labor leaders have an educational job to do on their own membership, and its success or failure may decide the future of unionism in this country.

An example of the failure of some unions to recognize that their success is dependent upon support from the black community came in a New York City teachers' strike. The black community supported the United Federation of Teachers in its previous strikes for more money and a bigger role in determining school policies. But in the fall of 1968, the teachers struck when a black-controlled local school board transferred some UFT members. Part of the ugliness of the dispute stemmed from the UFT's smear of the local board with loose charges of racism and anti-Semitism. So a union that had a record of close relations with black people plunged the city into a period of racial tension. It was obvious to all that a major reason for the strike was the union's desire to kill any prospects for a decentralized school system that would give power to locally elected boards of education. The UFT boasted of its strong civil rights record, but abandoned this concern when it came time to share actual power and privilege with blacks.

As the struggle for equality becomes more intense, it becomes harder to accept anything less than complete support from labor's leadership.

The backlash we are witnessing from some segments of the population is noticeably waning in the business community. Business, traditionally the most conservative area in American life, has taken steps to respond to the crisis of the cities. True, there have been many holdouts, and action doesn't always match good intentions, but in general the situation is encouraging.

Today's business leadership is the best trained and potentially the most responsive to its social obligations in our history. We have a new breed of businessmen today; the professional manager has replaced the family-dominated management of old, and he has brought with him a greater sophistication and knowledge of society. He is fully aware of business' dependence on expansionist economic policies of government, and he knows that the growth of large black populations in the cities is something that vitally concerns the nation and his company. In the past, business needed unskilled laborers and welcomed high unemployment, for it meant cheap labor. But today it knows that growth is dependent on an adequate supply of professional men, computer technicians, and men in a host of job classifications that didn't exist a decade ago. Business can no longer afford the waste of human talents and energies it once was able to tolerate.

For these and other reasons, some of the top businessmen in the country are taking the lead in opening up jobs for black people and in creating a social and economic climate that has no place for racism. Such people as Henry Ford and the leaders of the National Alliance of Businessmen are making a national effort to create jobs for black workers. Stanley Marcus and others refuse to buy supplies from businesses that discriminate. Many top businessmen are active in the Urban Coalition and in industry groups trying to solve the urban crisis. As a group, they are among the most committed people in America today.

But it is an uphill fight, for business in the past has so effectively excluded blacks from its ranks that it will take a massive effort to break through the racism that still permeates many of the hiring and promoting practices of American industry. Part of the problem lies in the inability of a $100,000 chief executive officer of a major corporation to understand fully the difficulties faced by black Americans, or even to comprehend the enormity of the effort required.

I recall a long talk I had with the president of one of the hundred largest companies in the country. He told me that he backed my idea of a domestic Marshall Plan for Black America, and he was critical of present inadequate efforts to end poverty. Ten years ago his fellow businessmen would have considered him a wild-eyed radical.

Then he started talking about the special efforts his company was making. As he went on it became clear to me that this man, though obviously sincere, didn't have the faintest idea what was required. The "wonderful programs" his company was sponsoring consisted of hiring a handful of Negro teenagers for summer jobs in only two of the fifty or sixty cities in which his company, with sales well into the hundreds of millions of dollars, did business.

Behind the facade of fine-sounding words and press releases, too many companies like his are doing next to nothing to fulfill their responsibilities. A study by the National Industrial Conference Board found a yawning gap between company policy and performance in employment of blacks. Few of the companies studied were doing as well as they wanted to, or even as well as the top brass thought they were doing. The study concluded that all the successful companies had one thing in common: "A chief executive determined that the program produce results, and willing to commit himself to its success for an indefinite period of time."

All too often a company president will send a memo around to his staff calling for more hiring of black workers, only to have middle-management executives throw it in the waste basket and forget about it. And even in companies where there is follow-through, thousands of man-hours of planning go out the window as an $80-a-week receptionist in personnel asks a Negro job applicant "What do you want, boy?"

Businessmen have to understand that achieving racially representative work forces, especially at white-collar levels, is going to take time and effort. It will mean holding executives responsible for fair employment in their departments, just as they are held responsible for sales and production levels. It will mean working with agencies such as the Urban League to recruit and train black people who never saw the inside of an office before. And it will mean developing a sensitivity to the problems of the black worker from the ghetto, perhaps even helping him with the housing, health, and educational needs that weigh on his mind and drain his energies.

Business has a responsibility to make this special effort

not only because its future prosperity depends upon it, but also because business, more than any other institution, created and profited from the ghetto. Business quietly tolerated school systems supported by its taxes which failed to train ghetto youngsters to function in the business world. It encouraged the housing segregation that keeps black workers concentrated in slums far from the jobs they need. It conscientiously pursued "white only" hiring policies. Every time progressive social legislation or civil rights laws were proposed, business leaders and trade associations fought them tooth and nail. Because of this the cities—business' markets —are becoming poorer and blacker. Federal action in job discrimination has come about because industry failed to lower its color bar voluntarily.

Many companies are still skilled at keeping blacks out of their offices. In 1967, the Equal Employment Opportunity Commission conducted a study of white-collar employment in New York City-based headquarters staffs of 100 of the largest corporations in the country. They found that a mere 2.6 per cent of these jobs were held by black workers. The reason for industry's credibility gap in the ghetto becomes obvious when we read that companies "who have *not* participated in the Plans for Progress organization [i.e., made voluntary fair-hiring pledges] have a record of higher minority utilization, in almost every occupational category, than those who have made these pledges." In another report on 4249 New York City businesses, the EEOC found that nearly half had no Negro white-collar employees at all.

Many companies hide behind a wall of stiff tests designed to screen out black applicants for jobs. Like the tests given by some unions, these have a strong white middle-class culture bias. They play down actual job requirements and emphasize verbal achievements beyond the reach of graduates of inferior ghetto schools. The EEOC investigated one complaint by a black worker who flunked a test for a job as a forklift operator. Here are three questions from the test, one that is widely used:

  1. *Clutter, clatter.* Do these words have a similar meaning? Contradictory? Mean neither the same nor opposite?
  2. *Piteous, pitiable.* Do these words have a similar meaning? Contradictory? Mean neither the same nor opposite?
  3. *Parasite, parasol.* Do these words have a similar meaning? Contradictory? Mean neither the same nor opposite?

The absurdity of such tests is demonstrated by the fact that the man who failed it had driven a forklift for five years for the federal government and scored 90 per cent on a government test on the operation of the machine.

I believe that the punishment should fit the crime: all company executives who use culturally biased tests like the one above should have *their* jobs depend on passing what is humorously called the "chitlin' test," devised by an antipoverty worker to show that such bias can work two ways. It's a test that a ghetto dropout could pass because it deals with *his* cultural background. Three sample questions:

  1. If a man is called a "blood," then he is—(a) a fighter, (b) a Mexican-American, (c) a Negro, (d) a hungry hemophile, (e) a red man or Indian.
  2. Cheap chitlings will taste rubbery unless they are cooked

long enough. How soon should you quit cooking them to eat and enjoy them? 45 minutes, 2 hours, 24 hours?

3. A "gas head" is a person who has—(a) a fast-moving car, (b) stable of "lace," (c) "process," (d) habit of stealing cars, (e) long jail record for arson.

Black college graduates who apply for management-trainee positions are subjected to the psychological tests so popular these days. The white "experts" who conduct these tests don't seem to realize that certain character traits deemed unsuitable are actually *most* suitable for black men. One young qualified Negro was rejected for a good job because the tests showed him "somewhat bitter" and "cautious in human relations." If that's not normal behavior for a black man in the white world, I don't know what is. Without these traits the black man would never have survived.

But even the best companies—those that go into the ghetto to recruit workers and those that are not satisfied with a token black face near the door—lack sensitivity to the outlook of black workers. I spent weeks pressuring one man to start a large-scale hiring program. After its apparently successful beginning, he called me to say that problems were developing.

"Some of the new workers didn't show after payday," he said. "And lots of them come in late on Monday mornings. Just about everybody is at least a few minutes late every morning. What's going wrong?"

A little investigation showed that people were coming in late because they lived in the ghetto at the other end of town, and public transportation in the black ghetto was, as is usually the case, poor. The company helped organize car pools, and found homes in white areas near the plant for some of the men. Some of the people who quit did so because of racist heckling by bigoted foremen or co-workers.

The rest posed a different kind of problem. They just didn't believe the company really meant to give them a fair shake. The black workers saw no black foremen, no black supervisors, no black company officials. It was clear to them that they couldn't hope to get the promotions and the raises that made the job worthwhile; it looked like just another dead end. Black ballplayers are never late to the ballpark and never miss a plane because they know that Willie Mays makes $125,000 a year; they know that blacks are at the top of their profession. Black workers have to see black people at the top too.

The company president who called me realized this, but couldn't find a qualified Negro to handle top operations in management. I don't question his sincerity here; blacks have been so thoroughly excluded from positions where they could gain business experience that the few people qualified to hold vice-presidencies in a corporation of that size already had jobs they wouldn't leave. So we helped him on that problem too. A Negro was appointed to head a newly organized Urban Affairs Department; a black doctor took a top spot in the medical department; black business-school graduates were recruited and are being groomed for top management posts; and the company will soon place a black man on its board of directors. That company no longer has any special problems with lateness or absenteeism.

*It can be done.* All it takes is commitment by top business leadership: leadership with guts and determination.

# BEYOND RACISM

The racial ghetto didn't just happen—it was created by the deliberate racism of the federal government and the private real estate industry. The excuse given for housing discrimination has been economic—property values are supposed to go down when Negroes move into neighborhoods. But this has been proved false so often that it can exist only as an ill-disguised rationalization of the sickness of racism.

A study of residential areas in Oakland, including some that had Negro families for the first time, showed that not a single area suffered a drop in property values between 1950 and the 1960 census. In a segregated neighborhood that had only 4 Negroes among 769 families in 1950, homes were valued at $11,789. Ten years later the neighborhood was integrated—101 Negro families, 935 white families—and its homes were valued at $19,000, *a 60 per cent increase*. By contrast, in an "exclusive" area that remained lily-white, property values rose only 30 per cent, some 15 per cent less than the average for the city, and only half the increase enjoyed by the newly integrated neighborhood.

The federally sponsored ghetto slum got its big boost from the Federal Housing Administration in the 1930s and 1940s. FHA manuals stipulated that "properties shall continue to be occupied by the same social and racial group" as a condition of government backing for mortgages. The FHA warned its mortgage valuators against "adverse influences" such as "inharmonious racial groups" and strongly recommended using restrictive covenants "since these provide the surest protection against undesirable encroachment." FHA even provided a model covenant for use by bigots too ignorant to write one themselves.

FHA also "red-lined" areas that weren't eligible for its services, supposedly because these areas were older and therefore more of an insurance risk. Most often the borders of the red-lined district perfectly coincided with the borders of the black ghetto—the very area most in need of FHA insurance and services. Private insurance companies kept their own red-lined maps, so the growing ghettos became economically doomed to deterioration.

At the same time the federal government was encouraging segregation, it was helping to sponsor the massive white exodus to suburbia. FHA and the Veterans Administration financed $120 billion worth of new housing—only 2 per cent of it to black families. The result has been to turn the cities into vast black ghettos in a sea of white suburbs. Today, 80 per cent of all new housing is going up in suburbs into which Negroes are still not welcome. Racial discrimination in most housing is now illegal, but zoning regulations which stipulate lot size, and therefore price, provide legal economic barriers to replace the illegal racial barriers.

But federal generosity to middle-class whites is not limited to helping them afford homes in all-white suburbs; it also builds the roads that make their move possible. More than $40 billion has been spent on subsidized roads that let white commuters speed past the ghetto, moving from their white neighborhoods to their white offices in a separate world from which the black man has been effectively excluded.

A government so intent on subsidizing its rich and its middle class might also consider subsidizing its poor, but even programs supposedly designed to help low-income fam-

ilies have been used to benefit other segments of the population, or have been ineffective.

Urban renewal, for example, was widely touted as the
program that would replace slums with decent housing.
What it has done is replace homes occupied by Negro families with luxury housing and office buildings. The guiding
philosophy has not been "How can we build more homes for
the poor?" but "How can we get blacks out of the valuable
parts of downtown areas?"

Urban renewal often means Negro removal. Nearly
400,000 housing units were destroyed in urban renewal
projects. They were replaced by only about 100,000 new
units, including a mere 25,000 that were within the price
range of the low-income families displaced, more than two
thirds of whom were black. Washington, D.C., destroyed a
predominately Negro slum housing 23,500 people and replaced it with a spanking-new development housing about
15,000 people at rents that range to $400 per month. A
study of displaced tenants found that for more than one out
of three Negro tenants, rent for their new homes ate up over
a third of their incomes. In the past twenty-five years Chicago has displaced 200,000 people, more than 80 per cent of
them black, to make way for urban renewal developments
and expressways. Only 3100 found new apartments in public housing; the rest pay an average of $22 a month more
than they used to.

Other government programs promise far more than they
deliver. The rent supplement program has a tenant pay 25
per cent of his income for rent, with government subsidies
making up the difference, but only 12,000 units covered by
this program were started in 1968. The 221(d)3 program lets

nonprofit sponsors of housing borrow at below market interest rates, but very few moderate-income families benefit, and rents remain too high for the poor.

Public housing is the obvious way to house people too poor to afford decent housing in the open market. The Commission on Urban Housing estimates the need for such low-income housing at 700,000 to 900,000 units per year, but only 800,000 units have been built in all of the thirty-five years we have had public housing. Although New York has over 100,000 people on its waiting list for public housing (and other cities have long waiting lists too), a mere 46,000 public housing units were started in *all* cities in 1968.

Washington, D.C., offers a perfect example of the unmet needs for public housing. Half the city's population can't afford decent private housing; 40 per cent now pay more than they can afford for rent; 100,000 children (70 per cent of them black) are growing up in overcrowded conditions; and 75,000 children are in families too poor to pay even the minimum rents in public housing projects.

Most public housing is simply a federally sponsored ghetto, thanks to the apathy of federal officials and the racism of local housing authorities. Special efforts were made to locate projects in the heart of the ghetto, and not until 1968 did the government warn it would no longer approve such official apartheid practices. But about 70 per cent of public housing buildings are occupied exclusively by members of one race or the other, and local authorities still plan projects for overcrowded ghetto areas that lack adequate facilities to service existing populations. Sometimes there is even segregation within a project. Boston's Mission Hill Project consists of two sets of buildings run by a single manager. One set is all white, the other—across the street —is nearly all black. The U.S. Civil Rights Commission pointed out that there are even separate windows for the two in the Project's rental offices; all that's needed is to put up signs saying WHITE and COLORED and the office could be in the heart of Mississippi.

Even federal and local tax laws help create slum ghettos. A study prepared for the National Commission on Urban Problems states: "As the Federal income tax is now constituted, the profitable course for real estate investors is to take accelerated depreciation after purchase, avoid repairs, and sell off their properties within a decade before their tax shelter fades. Continuity of ownership and sound maintenance are inhibited by opportunities for fast gains in this cycle of constant trading." The cycle results in higher rents for deteriorating apartments as well. Local property taxes and higher assessments for buildings in which improvements are made also discourage owners from keeping up their properties.

But we can't blame Washington for everything. The private real estate industry has done more to create two separate societies than any other industry. The group that speaks for the country's 84,000 realtors is the National Association of Real Estate Boards. Until 1950 its Code of Ethics warned against "introducing into a neighborhood . . . members of any race or nationality, or any individuals whose presence will clearly be detrimental to property values." Its most recent code includes an amendment that reads: "The Realtor should not be instrumental in introducing into a neighborhood a character or property or use which will clearly be detrimental to property values in that neighborhood." Although the word *race* no longer appears, the meaning is still clear to all. The NAREB also called the open-housing bill, which eventually passed over its objections, "an immoral doctrine." The use of the word *immoral* and the incorporation of racist strictures in a Code of *Ethics* are indicative of a curious mentality.

Racism can be highly profitable for the individual realtor. Many a "transitional" neighborhood has been quickly absorbed into the ghetto because of unscrupulous blockbusting techniques. After a Negro has moved onto the block, his new neighbors are swamped by calls from persistent real estate agents who play on their fears to encourage them to sell, often at panic-induced low prices. The houses are then resold to blacks at far higher than market prices, providing a quick profit for the realtor, illegally converting what might have become an integrated community into a ghetto.

Housing segregation is not only self-perpetuating, creating ever-larger, ever-more dilapidated slums, but it also makes the understanding gap between the races more difficult to bridge. The unbridled fear that is unleashed when open housing is brought up results from the stereotypes of Negroes held by white people who have never had enough interracial contacts to be able to see Negroes as people and as potential good neighbors. Prisoners of their own stereotypes, many whites flee, leaving their children in turn a legacy of fear and unreason.

And often the flight is costly. A black policeman who lives in an integrated housing development told a reporter about a white colleague who is a John Bircher:

This man was saying that if all Negroes were like me there'd be no problem but because of the kind that were moving in, he'd bought a house on the Island. It was a long boring commute, the house always needed repair, the mortgage was a strain on his budget. When I told him what my carrying charges are at Rochdale, how big the rooms are, how close it is, and what the community affords us and our children, he was flabbergasted. And envious.

"Well," I told him, "you're paying a penalty of approximately fifty dollars a month for fleeing. You want to segregate yourself, and so you're depriving your family of the kind of vacation that mine is going to be able to take next summer with our housing savings. And you don't even give yourself the chance to find out that there are other Negroes like me."

White Power, to many in Black America, is symbolized by the police. No other group arouses so much hostility in the ghetto, and often with good cause. Most of the riots were triggered by a police action, relatively innocuous by itself, but symbolic of the way many policemen have treated black people. Blacks have some justification for viewing the police with suspicion: in the South they enforced racist laws and oppressed Negroes; in the North, they allow ghetto crime to flourish while often abusing black people.

It's too bad that such generalizations damage the majority of decent policemen who suffer for the misdeeds or racist attitudes of the minority. Although we here discuss the shortcomings of many police departments around the country, we must bear in mind that most policemen are decent, hard-working individuals who are sometimes ill-equipped to do the demanding, complex job society has charged them with.

Police brutality has become something of a cliché. While

physical brutality exists, many more blacks feel the weight of what we might call police humiliation. An overbearing manner, a refusal to show the least politeness, an attitude of fear mixed with hostility that lets black people know that this man with a uniform and a gun sees them as somewhat less than human.

The extent of racism among police officers in the ghetto is staggering. A University of Michigan study found: "In predominately Negro precincts over three-fourths of the white policemen expressed prejudiced or highly prejudiced attitudes toward Negroes. Only one per cent of the officers expressed attitudes which could be described as sympathetic toward Negroes. Indeed, close to one-half of all the officers in the predominately Negro high-crime areas show extreme prejudice against Negroes."

Judge George Edwards, himself a former police commissioner (of Detroit), writes that "policemen in the North and South become deeply imbued with the idea that the major part of their responsibility was to keep the Negro in his place ... often did not heed to distinguish between law-abiding and lawless Negroes." Small wonder that so many blacks view the police as White America's army of occupation.

A related problem is the emotional stability of police officers who must work in the hostile ghettos. Only one out of four police departments tests applicants for emotional fitness. Portland, Oregon, which has such tests, found that 25 per cent of applicants fail such screening. If this is typical, then many cities without adequate testing procedures are arming and sending into our streets emotionally unstable individuals. But even tests for emotional stability pass people with bigoted racial views. In Portland, the police union went to court in an attempt to stop the police commissioner from implementing a program designed to add more Negroes to the five already on the force. Like Portland's, most police departments are almost lily-white, and black officers are relegated to lower ranks. The Kerner Commission found that:

- One in every 26 Negroes is a sergeant; the white ratio is one in 12.
- One in every 114 Negroes is a lieutenant; the white ratio is one in 26.
- One in every 235 Negroes is a captain or above; the white ratio is one in 53.

Although the relations between the black community and the police are the single most crucial factor in many cities, few police departments make any serious effort to reduce tensions. Those that do maintain community-relations programs give them very low priorities. Lieutenant Dante Andreotti resigned from San Francisco's police force after his attempts to make his community-relations program a success floundered under the attacks from the rest of the force. His men were taunted as "nigger-lovers" by other policemen.

The police in general [Andreotti told *Fortune*] look upon community relations as something of minor importance. They regard it as something they want to do out of their hearts. They want to be efficient. You can get technically efficient as hell, but if you are not effective with people you might as well close shop. Our war was with the police department. We were never successful in getting the message down to the foot soldier: that community relations is the most important job.

I sincerely believe that policemen are hung up on this law-and-order bit. They forget the law part. Too many of them regard the law as something that they impose upon the people and not as something that protects people's rights. Too many policemen feel they have to show they are the boss on the street. Instead of trying to communicate with the Negro, to make him feel that the law is for him too, they are busy espousing the thin-blue-line theory, the idea that they stand between you and chaos. The system itself contributes to the cynicism, the feeling of isolation, that many policemen have.

If the police place a low priority on community relations, they also often place a low priority on law enforcement in the ghetto. Criminal activity, prostitution, and dope sales that would be stopped elsewhere in the city are tolerated in the ghetto. The U.S. Commission on Civil Rights reports that the Cleveland police took almost four times as long to respond to calls reporting robbery in the ghetto as for the (white) district where response was next lowest. A Boston minister told the Commission that "One family had called the police because of an incident in the area. They waited . . . twenty minutes and there was no response. Then someone was smart enough to think of calling the police, saying 'Get out here quick, there is a Negro beating up a white man.' The police were there in two minutes."

Police lawlessness is another cause of the ghetto's hostility toward policemen. Middle-class Americans may be shocked when an occasional case of police misconduct comes to their attention but many children in the ghetto have seen policemen accepting payoffs from gamblers and dope peddlers.

Bribery probably exists elsewhere, but because of the contempt many policemen feel for black people, police lawlessness is open and visible in the ghetto. A study of police activity in slum areas made for the President's Commission on

Law Enforcement and Administration of Justice by the University of Michigan's Bureau of Social Research, reported that 27 per cent of the policemen studied either were observed in or admitted to "some form of misconduct that could be classified as a felony or a misdemeanor." The findings are even more stunning because the misconduct occurred under the eyes of observers who were placed in police cars or went along on foot patrol with the policemen. Even though the observers were present, policemen took bribes, stole from burglarized stores, shook down violators, perjured themselves in court, and protected illegal establishments. Some even admitted that they carried extra weapons with them to enable them "to argue self-defense" if they injured a citizen and there was no weapon used by the citizen.

Racial tensions are increased by police hostility toward black militant groups. Often the police conduct undeclared wars against them, goading extremists in an attempt to force them into situations where the policeman could use justified violence against them. Dr. John P. Spiegel, director of the Lemberg Center for the Study of Violence, stated: "To the Irish, Italian, or Polish police officer of working class background, black-skinned activists and youthful protesters are the embodiment of everything that is alien, evil, and destructive of the American social system. Militant youths and black militants are perceived not only as un-American, but also as nonhuman. Ruled out of the human race, they become unpersons and therefore deserving of intense attack, as one would attack a rattlesnake."

In New York, a mob of 150 men, including many out-of-uniform, off-duty policemen, viciously attacked a group of twelve black militants and white youths *inside a courthouse*. Small wonder then that former Attorney-General Ramsey

Clark said the most dangerous type of violence was police action "in excess of authority," for "who will protect the public when the police violate the law?"

Partly, the problem of police violence stems from undue emphasis placed on the violent aspect of police work. Most departments automatically promote patrolmen who are involved in gun battles and tend to ignore imaginative police work such as heading off riot situations by cool-headed action or conducting investigations that solve crimes. Another failing seems to be the fostering of the myth that the policeman is a soldier in a dangerous war against crime and is daily risking his life. To a degree, of course, it is true that police work is very dangerous, but most policemen spend most of their time on activities unconnected with crime, such as directing traffic or returning lost children. In New York City firemen had three times more injuries and sanitation men had four times more injuries than policemen. Measured by days of work lost, the injuries suffered by firemen and sanitation men seemed to be more serious.

The majority of policemen are honest, dedicated men trying to do a good job under difficult conditions. They are too often blamed for a system they didn't make, and for the misdeeds of their fellow officers. Sometimes this leads to a senseless lack of cooperation from the people they are trying to protect. But their job is made harder when other citizens protect wrongdoers in uniform. The kind of knee-jerk reflex support of every policeman or police action, no matter what the circumstance, only hurts the cause of good law enforcement.

White America refuses to look at the failings of its police, in part because it views them as its only protection from the black hordes bent on crime and destruction. But this is also a racist myth. Crime in America is as segregated as the rest of our lives. In 1967, the President's Commission on Law Enforcement and Administration of Justice, on which I served, issued a report that was probably the most exhaustive analysis of crime ever made. Our conclusion was that white people are most likely to commit offenses against other whites; Negroes against other Negroes.

We found that less than one out of ten aggravated assaults was interracial and that crimes of violence, including murder and rape, most often occur between people who know each other. In Washington, D.C., a high-crime area with a total population that is two-thirds Negro, only 12 out of 172 murders were interracial and 80 per cent of all rapes involved persons of the same race.

Middle-class Americans seem obsessed by "crime in the streets," but the real victims are the poor. The Commission found that people earning less than $3000 per year are four times as likely to be the victims of rape and five times as likely to be robbed as those earning more than $10,000. And crime's victims are more likely to be black. Negroes are four times as likely to be robbed as white persons. A black man in Chicago is six times as likely to be assaulted or robbed as a white man; a black woman is eight times as likely to be raped, robbed, or assaulted as a white woman. These figures document the high amount of violence and crime in the ghettos, just as there was more crime in the slums that housed other ethnic groups. Crime is spawned by poverty, hopelessness, and the anger that goes with feeling trapped and discriminated against. The statistics argue the need for better police protection in the ghetto.

But the Commission also found that those who often scream loudest about "crime in the streets" are those who commit crimes themselves. When we sampled 1700 adults at random, 91 per cent of them admitted to offenses for which they could have received a jail sentence. Some of our most "respectable" people commit such "clean" crimes as fraud, consumer cheating, embezzlement, petty thievery at their offices, and price-fixing deals, all of which cost the nation more than three times as much in lost property as crimes such as robbery and theft.

Among the most profound failures of White America are those of its newspapers, advertisers, and broadcasters. An FCC commissioner has charged the broadcasting industry with building "more walls than bridges between the white and black communities of our cities." It is precisely because our mass media have immense power to change men's minds that their failure looms so large. They have not used their ability to cure the sickness of racism by educating their viewers and readers to the realities of American life.

A casual reader of newspapers would assume that Negroes never die, never marry, and never work; that they do riot, commit crime, and excel in sports. Black people never make the papers unless they do something dramatic or startling, preferably of an illegal nature. The day-to-day life of the ghetto, unlike that of White America, is ignored and Negroes are portrayed as two-dimensional figures apart from the total community. The racism of the press mirrors the racism of its readers. Because of this, the media have helped to perpetuate the ghetto and have increased the understanding gap that plagues whites and blacks in this country.

Much has changed since the Kerner Commission's Report indicted the press for its sensationalistic approach to racial news; many newspapers and broadcasting stations have reversed their previous practices. Black people get more balanced coverage now, and quite a few television programs have added black actors to their casts, while many advertisers have taken to showing Negroes who have headaches or own cars in their commercials. But blacks still remain peripheral and unreal figures on television, added as an afterthought to give a touch of color to the unrelieved whiteness of the home screen.

That problems still remain does not reflect the lack of the will to change, but rather an inability to understand the processes of social change that are engulfing us all. Reporters and editors alike can't seem to get beyond the reporting of spot news to inform the public of the larger meaning of the news events they cover in such detail. Perhaps the biggest story of our times is the new determination of black people to control the institutions that affect their lives, not because of a hunger for power, but because those institutions have created the misery and despair of ghetto life. But the press persists in covering this story of profound social change as if it were just another police story—local government versus the angry blacks.

School decentralization is one of the top issues in many cities, and it will become even more so. When New York's teachers went on strike last year because a decentralized school district transferred some teachers, the press was filled for days with news of charges and countercharges, police action and demonstrations. The real issues were buried in a mass of newsprint and television footage that consistently missed the point of why the community insisted on controlling its schools and of the deep social changes that were taking place. The public wallowed in ignorance, as did the reporters who helped to spread misunderstanding.

The press (that includes the electronic press of television and radio) stresses the obvious and the sensational because it cannot understand the deeper significance of what appears to be commonplace. Telling the story of daily life in the ghetto, showing how racism works to trap black hopes, and telling the stories of people who overcame discrimination and poverty to succeed is *the* story of our times. It may not be as sensational as some self-proclaimed militant cursing "whitey" but it is of profoundly greater significance.

The press creates monsters, then blames Negroes for them. We get all sorts of editorials advising Negroes not to follow people we never heard of before the press started building them up. Almost every angry young man on a street corner becomes "a Negro spokesman" in the morning papers.

Sometimes black people enjoy making the press look foolish. I recall that, at a meeting of a small group of people in Harlem, a lawyer told us he could make the front pages. When we asked him how, he said he would call a press conference and announce the formation of a Negro political party. We all laughed and didn't think any more about it until a few days later when, sure enough, there was the story splashed all over page one.

Reporters and editors are often themselves victims of the understanding gap—middle-class white suburbanites only a little more sophisticated than their neighbors and with little understanding of what it means to be black and poor in a white and affluent society. The discriminatory policies that help keep blacks out of the newsrooms of America mean that many newspapers have no way to communicate with black Americans. A 1967 survey of 300 newspapers found only 119 Negro reporters, and no editorial writers. Less than a third of the papers said they were willing to train Negroes for jobs. Only 3.4 per cent of the jobs in the broadcasting industry are held by black people, with most blacks in subordinate positions. Less than 1 per cent of editors and supervisors are Negroes, and most of them work for Negro-owned newspapers—newspapers that are being raided now by a white press anxious to improve its image by hiring instant Negroes, rather than by training promising young black people.

The press' record is one of failure: It has failed to present an accurate picture of the American racial crisis; it has alienated its Negro readers; it has excluded Negroes from its ranks; and it has accepted the racism that so distorts our national life. The Kerner Commission's indictment still holds true: "It is the responsibility of the news media to tell the story of race relations in America, and with notable exceptions, the media have not yet turned to the task with the wisdom, sensitivity, and expertise it demands."

Perhaps the most hypocritical and immoral institution in American life is the one that presumes to set the standards for our society: the church. In a time of moral conflict the organized churches present a picture of smug complacency as they tolerate or even condone the sin of racism. Some churches so completely mirror their members' bigotry that their credo might be "I am my black brother's keeper; I keep him in his place."

Timid men preside over congregations that may be willing to donate money to missions in Africa but will not permit black people to come to the church to pray. Eleven o'clock

# WHITE AMERICA

on Sunday morning is still the most segregated hour in America.

The church has failed to bring its purported message of love and brotherhood to its own members. One recent study of church members found that "... nearly half say they would move if several Negro families moved into their block. A third think Negroes less intelligent; nearly half blame Communists and other radicals for racial tension."

Churches have not only failed to counter this moral rot in their midst, they have sometimes actually encouraged it. How can an institution that claims to foster brotherhood so consistently turn its back on the poor and the dispossessed? Church schools have become a haven for parents who pull their children out of integrated public schools in order to keep them in a lily-white atmosphere.

Religious institutions have assets of well over $80 billion, and that does not include investment profits, dividends, and rents—all tax free. Americans contribute $5 billion a year to churches, and religious institutions spend over a billion dollars every year on new facilities. The churches could use their economic power to create jobs and opportunities for the poor and the black, but in most cases they remain as indifferent and as immoral as the rest of White America.

This un-Christian smugness and tolerance of evil has led many, especially the young, to abandon the church. And it is leading to revolt within the church itself, as young ministers rebel against the pious platitudes of the establishment. The most creative and committed young ministers and priests feel that their calling should have a higher purpose than pulling in donations for a building fund while the cities are havens of misery and poverty. Dedicated churchmen and laymen alike know that unless the churches become relevant

(133)

to the burning questions of our time—questions that are deeply moral ones—the church will become an anachronism.

Several of the largest denominations have recognized this and have officially committed themselves to working for equality. But their high-sounding statements have not yet been translated into effective action. Aside from encouraging some "urban ministries" and occasionally increasing donations to ghetto projects, the churches have not matched their deeds to their press releases.

An indication of how the power of religious institutions could be used is Project Equality, a plan for church groups to buy only from firms that give employment opportunities to minorities. Some church groups have formed foundations to encourage black businesses and to help organize ghetto communities. These are hopeful developments in an otherwise dismal picture.

If the church is to survive, it must become responsive to the growing numbers of young people and young clergymen who don't give a damn about its traditional concept of morality, a concept that is more concerned with the degree of nudity in a movie than the degree of despair in a slum. The urban and racial crisis is in its most profound sense a moral crisis, and the churches cannot ignore it.

One of New York's landmarks is the Cathedral Church of St. John the Divine, the world's largest Gothic cathedral. Its unfinished dome, shrouded by scaffolding, looks down on the slums of Harlem. And it will remain unfinished "until there is greater evidence that the anguish and despair of our unadvantaged people has been relieved." That unfinished dome is a symbol for America's churches and for all of us, a symbol of our unfinished task: to create an Open Society. As a nation, we are morally crippled and our churches have a mission of moral healing that must take precedence over their other, less important concerns.

America's educational system was created not only to provide people with the skills needed by our society but also to transmit to young people society's values and beliefs. If we accept the fact that racism is one of our most cherished values, then the schools have succeeded admirably, for they, more than any other institution, have perpetuated racism and destroyed countless black children in the process.

Black children actually fall farther behind the longer they stay in school. Black sixth-graders are two and a half years behind white sixth-graders; by the time they have become seniors in high school the gap has grown to three and a half years. Educators like to think that this is the fault of the children, but the Head Start program has proved otherwise. Black three- and four-year-olds who got early schooling in the program actually did get a "head start," but once they fell into the clutches of the school system they lost their lead over youngsters who didn't get preschool training and proceeded on the treadmill of failure that awaits promising black children in our system of miseducation.

There are plenty of reasons for the failure of the schools to educate black youngsters, but all of them come down to the same basic racism that poisons the rest of American life. School districts refusing to implement the fifteen-year-old Supreme Court ruling that declared segregated schools unconstitutional set an example of lawlessness in a defense of racism.

Integration works. It is as valuable for white youngsters as it is.for black. In a world that is three quarters nonwhite, no white parent can afford the luxury of limiting his child's experience to all-white schools, classmates, and friends. Integrated schools work for black children, too. Studies show that their achievement is higher there than it is in all-black schools. That's because schools with majority white enrollments are favored by school boards and communities alike. They get the resources and the interest denied ghetto schools that are stigmatized as "inferior" and whose children—and their parents—are held in contempt.

But despite repeated demonstrations of the value of integrated schools, districts, North and South, go to extraordinary lengths to keep them segregated. Cincinnati, for example, bused children from an overcrowded black school past several predominately white schools to another nearly all-black school five and a half miles away. Federal investigators found that more than four out of five Cleveland schoolchildren go to schools that are over 95 per cent or more white or over 95 per cent Negro. Enforcement of the Supreme Court's ruling has been all but nonexistent, thanks to Congressional opposition, local resistance, and the lack of funds for enforcement. As the U.S. Commission on Civil Rights put it, "Racial isolation in the schools . . . is intense whether the cities are large or small, whether the proportion of Negro enrollment is large or small, whether they are located in the North or South."

So we are left with segregated schools and predominately black schools that are as unequal as they are separate. Black students get the worst schools, the least-trained teachers, and the worst equipment. Thirty Detroit ghetto schools were built in the administration of President Grant—a hundred years ago. Ghetto schools are not only older, they are also overcrowded. Over half of Chicago's predominately black high schools have enrollments more than 50 per cent *above* capacity, but less than a sixth of the predominately white high schools are that full. In city after city, thirty-five and forty black kids are crammed into each classroom in rotting buildings, while excess seating capacity goes unused in all-white schools elsewhere.

Black schools lack the facilities to teach children skills needed in today's technological world. Barely half of Washington's ghetto elementary schools have libraries. The Coleman Report of the U.S. Office of Education says that Negro pupils ". . . have less access to physics, chemistry and language laboratories; there are fewer books per pupil in their libraries; the textbooks are less often in sufficient supply."

From some of the textbooks I've seen, perhaps that lack isn't such a bad one after all. Our children—all of them, white and black—are being poisoned by textbooks that are either unrealistic or outright racist. History texts, especially, have wounded black children and lied to white kids with racist fantasies of a past that never was. This example comes from a book, *The Growth of the American Republic,* published in 1940 by two of the most famous historians of our time, Samuel Eliot Morison and Henry Steele Commager:

As for Sambo, whose wrongs moved the abolitionists to wrath and tears, there is some reason to believe that he suffered less than any other class in the South from its "peculiar institution." The majority of the slaves were adequately fed, well cared for, and apparently happy. . . . Although brought to America by force, the incurably optimistic Negro soon became attached to the country, and devoted to his "white folks."

Books such as this helped produce a nation of racists who believe that whites are superior to blacks. Small wonder Americans are shocked by the anger and pain that wells up from the ghetto's devoted "Sambos." When books take a more positive approach to the black people in our history, it is usually the "safe" black man whose life is taught— Booker T. Washington, who urged Negroes to reach an accommodation with White America, rather than Frederick Douglass or W. E. B. DuBois, who fought segregation and insisted on equal rights.

Racism is not confined to academic subjects. Black kids are crammed into vocational schools that are supposed to prepare them for skilled jobs, but don't. Outmoded equipment is used to teach skills that are becoming outmoded themselves. These schools are disaster areas, hothouses of frustration. The black dropout rate in ghetto schools is in the neighborhood of 50 per cent.

The massive amount of money needed to make these schools function is nowhere in sight. Cleveland spends $578 per pupil during the school year, suburban Cuyahoga Heights $1344. The Great Cities Program for School Improvement, made up of sixteen of the largest urban school districts in the country, stated: "Big city schools generally have two-thirds or less to spend per pupil than do the schools in the adjacent suburbs." White America's scarce educational resources are funneled into schools that contain white children, and the black children—for whom education is the only road out of poverty—get the leavings.

The disparity in resources even results in gnawing hunger for black children. Six million children qualify for free school lunches, but only a third get them. One St. Louis school has a thousand children from welfare families, but only a dozen get free lunches. The rest go hungry. Some of this hunger is caused by lack of facilities to prepare food in the ancient buildings that serve ghetto students. In Detroit, seventy-eight of the seventy-nine schools that have no lunch program because of lack of facilities are in the ghetto. Not one of Cleveland's elementary schools has its own lunch program.

Ghettto schools get the most inexperienced teachers and have the highest turnover rates. The average turnover in New York City teaching staffs is about 10 per cent; in East Harlem it is 20 to 25 per cent. In forty nearly all-black or Puerto Rican schools, half the teachers had less than three years' experience, double the rate for white schools. The slum child needs a host of special services as well as good teachers, but the average slum school has only forty professional staff members per thousand students; the suburban schools have seventy per thousand.

All of these facts and statistics measure the failure of White America to educate black youth, but the most pernicious element in the destruction of our children is the contempt in which they are held by the educational establishment. *Black kids fail because they are expected to fail and because the whole system of American education is designed to encourage their failure.*

Teaching staffs are often made up of people whose attitudes combine fear with ill-concealed contempt. Teachers are not immune to the racism of the society of which they are a part. If they expected their students to succeed and if they imparted to black students a sense of worth and dignity, *those children would succeed.* Ghetto children have to overcome not only the poverty and despair of the slums, but also systematic destruction of their ability to learn, a destruction that is fostered by the hostility of many of their own teachers and counselors.

A Harvard psychology professor has proved that teachers' attitudes affect the performance of their students. He conducted an experiment in a San Francisco elementary school with a large Mexican-American enrollment. All students were given an IQ test, then a random sampling of names was selected. Teachers were told that the test indicated which students were due to spurt ahead in achievement in the coming year. It wasn't true, of course, but the teachers believed it. A year later, the students were tested again. Sure enough, the ones picked at random actually did achieve better scores; in the earlier grades they scored IQ gains more than double those of other children.

Why? Because their teachers actually believed they would achieve this, thanks to the false information they had been given. In hundreds of little ways during that school year, they conveyed that belief to their students and encouraged them to do better. Children who had been neglected were called on to answer classroom questions and a wrong answer didn't result in "That's all right, Johnny, you just don't know better," but in "Sure you know the answer to that one," followed by a hint or a word of encouragement. For some of the children, it was the first time in their entire school experience that a teacher had really cared about their performance.

It is clear from this, and from other experiments in the behavioral sciences, that among the black child's greatest obstacles in learning are his own teacher, his principal, and the whole apparatus of an educational bureaucracy that doesn't believe that black kids are able to (or even that they ought to) learn.

Like much of American racism, these attitudes need not be blatant, in fact they often exist despite protestations of how much the child is loved and respected. But the same defensive mechanism that has enabled black people to survive through 350 years of racism operates like a radar system to detect prejudiced attitudes. Children can detect in a raised eyebrow, in the tone of a voice, in a chance remark a whole range of nuances that tells them they are unwanted and uncared for.

The schools, once the vehicle for Americanizing millions of immigrant children and preparing them for success in our society, have become instruments of destruction for black children. The tragedy of this state of affairs is deepened by the realization that the children of the ghetto are so thirsty for knowledge, so hungry for the success their fathers never knew. These kids exhibit a resiliance, an aliveness, an inner strength that the schools could so easily build on. Instead of becoming obsessed with the problems involved, educators must realize that a whole generation of ghetto youth could blossom forth if they would but believe in their students and build on their strengths, strengths that would make it possible for them to survive in a hostile world that would wither lesser spirits.

Dr. John J. Fischer, president of Teachers College at Columbia University, has defined a good school as ". . . one where children know they are welcome and respected, where every day they experience some measure of success, and where they are constantly reminded that what they do really makes a difference."

Such schools do exist in the ghetto—but often outside the regular public school system. The Urban League, for example, established a network of street academies in New York —storefront schools—staffed by street workers who recruit dropouts. The youngsters are motivated to learn and get the remedial help they need to bring themselves up to grade level. But our aim is to show that youngsters pushed out of the incompetent public schools of the ghetto are as capable of going to college as suburban students. Street-academy graduates are placed at prep schools, including the Urban League-sponsored Harlem Prep. Every one of Harlem Prep's 1968 graduating class of seventy was placed in college, an extraordinary record unmatched by the most prestigious schools in the country. Yet these are the same young people who were branded uneducable by the mind-destroying system that crushes black youth.

The success of the street-academy program shows what can be done when schools are bold, imaginative, and responsive to the communities they serve. Even the barrier of race falls. On one visit to Harlem Prep, I talked with a young man who was bitterly antiwhite. "But what about your teacher," I asked. "She's white, yet you get along beautifully with her." "Oh," he answered, "she's not white, she's nice." For this youngster, and for many thousands of others trapped in the slum ghettos of urban America, "white" has taken on connotations of evil, racism, and oppression.

Such an outlook is at least understandable when we consider the way black Americans have been victimized by

# WHITE AMERICA

White Power. It is as if White America has been waging all-out war on black people for the past 350 years.

It would be a tragic mistake, however, for black attitudes to harden to the point where white society is totally written off as past redemption. American democracy has proved time and again that its apparent rigidity can be cast off, that it is flexible enough to change in the face of pressures. There are in America millions of white people who are just as outraged at racist practices as the angriest black people. I've traveled to just about every major city in the country in the past year or so, and everywhere I go I meet people anxious to work for an Open Society, determined to bring about a rebirth of a nation dedicated to the ideals of democracy for all its citizens.

We have to recognize this strength in White America and build on it. Blanket indictments of "whitey" won't bring freedom to the black man. Our job is to maintain contact with the decent, responsible white people in our society and help them to change the institutions that oppress us both.

I think America's greatest hope for the future lies in its young people. They are fed up with the hypocrisies of an adult society they can no longer respect. They seek a newer world, a brighter future. I have visited hundreds of colleges and everywhere I find the same response—an intense interest in and sympathy for the black revolution coupled with cynicism and a contempt for the institutions in our society that perpetuate racism. It is no accident that some of the rebellious student groups have said that "students are niggers." They recognize that society has exploited them and degraded them just as it has, to an immeasurably greater extent, black people. And behind the student unrest are demands that bear great resemblance to those of the ghetto. "Students are approaching the Establishment," wrote one Stanford student, "trying to discover if they can chart their own destiny, if they can have greater control over it. One of the themes on our campus might be termed 'impotent outrage.' We want so badly to have an impact on the society in which we live."

Their immediate confrontations have been with their parents and with their universities, but I expect they will also turn outward to fight the larger battles of changing our society. We saw the beginnings of this last year, when young people shaved their beards to be "clean for Gene" and nearly overturned the traditional political structure by their zealous involvement in Senator Eugene McCarthy's primary campaigns. This vast, still untapped energy and idealism may yet bring America back to its long-forgotten democratic ideals.

After every speech I've ever given at a college, students have come up to me to tell me: "My dad is always preaching about not smoking pot or drinking or having sex just because everyone else does it. But how can he expect me to listen to him when I see him conforming to the prejudices of our neighbors? What right does he have to tell me about morals when he cheats on his expense account and belongs to a club that won't admit Negroes and treats his black employees like dirt? I can't talk to him any more." And the expression on their faces tells me that they *do* want to establish communications with their parents; they desperately want to respect them but they can't: not until their parents do something worthy of respect.

# WHITE AMERICA

A good friend of the Urban League is the chief executive officer of one of America's largest corporations. He told me how he packed for a trip he took with me, a speaking tour of ten cities. "Where are you going this week, Pop?" his college-age kids asked him.

"I'm going on a speaking tour with Whitney Young to raise some money for the Urban League," he answered.

They were incredulous. "What," they asked, "you aren't going to check on that merger deal out West? You're not going to check on those new plants you were going to visit?"

"No. I'm putting company business aside for the next two weeks and I'm going to do my best to see that the Urban League gets the support it needs for its programs in the ghetto."

"Whitney," he later told me, "I've never seen my kids look at me with such respect and understanding. I was finally talking their language. The fine home I've built for them, their cars, their schooling are all taken for granted. I was just Mister Moneybags, the guy they came to when they needed something. But now we are finally on the same wave length. They see I care for more than just business; they finally see me as a person with the same concerns and ideals they have."

For these young people, civil rights and social change are where the action is. It's remarkable how the children of affluence identify with people living in slums. At one southern school that didn't even allow Negroes in until about 1960, I talked with half a dozen students, white and black. The black youngsters voiced their bitterness and their rejection of the distorted values of white society. But the real surprise was the white students. They agreed with what the black kids were saying right down the line. "They're absolutely right," they said. The white students told me that they felt they had to earn the right to form a coalition with black Americans, but that they didn't have the experience that would qualify them to express and feel the extent of the despair and bitterness in the ghetto fully. They told me that they needed to be helped by black Americans to see this, and they hoped to be asked to cooperate so that, together, blacks and whites could build a better society.

I was moved by their sincerity and their obvious desire to overcome the limitations of their experience so that they could enter into a meaningful relationship with their black fellow students. They, and the hundreds like them who have said similar things to me, could easily turn their backs on decency and melt into the apathetic, amorphous mass of white Americans, who silently tolerate the injustice and brutality that mark our lives. But they don't. They are involved, and in every way they are setting moral standards for their parents to live up to.

Just before the 1968 March on Washington, I was in the office of a top executive discussing his company's personnel practices. He was very much upset about the Urban League's role in helping to organize the March. "That's not the way to do things," he said. "All that will happen is that you'll get a bunch of hippies and Reds down there. Negroes are going to have to learn to be patient, to learn that you can't hold these big demonstrations all the time." Then he went on and on about "Reds" and "hippies" and how much white people like himself have done "for Negroes." In the middle of his tirade—just at the point where he was really getting steamed up about young radicals—the phone rang. After a short conversation, he hung up the receiver and slumped into his seat, ashen-faced. He sat there in silence for a while, then he turned to me and said: "Mr. Young, that was my daughter at college. She called to tell me that she was joining a group from her school to go to the March on Washington."

That girl, and the generation she represents, may yet redeem the promise of America and help unite our separate, bleeding societies.

# CHAPTER THREE

# BUILDING AN OPEN SOCIETY

To pursue our present course will involve the continuing polarization of the American community and, ultimately, the destruction of basic democratic values.

Only a greatly enlarged commitment to national action —compassionate, massive and sustained, backed by the will and resources of the most powerful and richest nation on this earth—can shape a future that is compatible with the historic ideals of American society.

—REPORT OF THE NATIONAL ADVISORY COMMISSION
ON CIVIL DISORDERS

SOMEWHERE ALONG the way, America got lost. We strayed far from the equalitarian ideals that once made us a symbol of freedom to the world. These ideals can be reclaimed now only by an unprecedented national commitment to undo the past and create a new future.

Our goal must be to move beyond racism and create an Open Society—a society in which each human being can flourish and develop to the maximum of his God-given potential; a society in which ethnic and cultural differences are not stifled for montonous conformity; a pluralistic society, alive, creative, open to the marvel of self-discovery.

An Open Society is not merely an "integrated" society—one that grudgingly allows Negroes some of the privileges white people enjoy. An Open Society is, rather, one that offers choices and options. Some Negroes may prefer to live together for the psychological security that comes from close-knit enclaves that share similar traditions and culture—as just about every other ethnic group in America has done. But in an Open Society, the exercise of such a choice would not be penalized with inadequate services, discriminatory practices, and open hostility. It would be but one of many choices that individuals would be free to make within the framework of a pluralistic society.

And an Open Society would offer white people an escape from homogenized blandness, encouraging creative diversity among people. It would give all people the right to choose what to retain of their own heritage. This goes far beyond the limitations inherent in superficial and often condescending integration. In the context of positive pluralism, black people would enter the dominant white society with a sense of roots, aware that they are contributing something positive and important. By now, we ought to see the fatal flaws of the old melting-pot theory, which sought to strip people of culture and traditions in order to transform everyone into middle-class, white Anglo-Saxons. Black people have something unique and valuable to contribute to American society—as other groups before them—and their pride in their heritage is an important part of this. Freedom cannot be portioned out only to those willing to reject their heritage.

An Open Society has to be based on equality. This means neither the superficial "equality of opportunity" that gets so much lip service these days, nor does it mean an impossible equality of achievement that assumes everyone will do as well as everyone else, regardless of innate differences. The measure of equality has to be group achievement: when, in each group in our society, roughly the same proportion of people succeed and fail, then we will have true equality.

Too many people assume that because laws have been passed and some doors have been opened, Negroes have equal opportunities. They ignore the brutal facts of life: that blacks are locked into slum ghettos without the economic and educational resources to compete on an equal basis. So long as black people are at a disproportionate disadvantage in jobs, health, education, and housing, equal opportunity is a cruel myth. You can't set a handicapped man and an Olympic sprinter on the same starting line and expect an equal race.

## BUILDING AN OPEN SOCIETY

During the Watts riots a reporter cornered a young man in the street and asked him why he was rioting, what did he want. "Mister," replied the youth, "I want what you just left to come here to ask me that question"—in other words, the things white middle-class Americans take for granted.

Building a truly Open Society will require, for a time at least, allocating *unequal* resources to enable *all* Americans to compete on an equal basis. This idea shocks some people, who complain it means "preferential treatment," ignoring the fact that it is because white people got preferential treatment for all these years that we have reached the present dangerous imbalance in society. The child of college-educated parents who grows up in financial security in an upper-middle-class home and in the kind of emotional security a pleasant suburban town provides has a tremendous head start in life. This start is denied to a black child whose mother is on welfare and who grows up in a decaying tenement. We've got to equalize the opportunities so that both those kids have the same chance for a fruitful, productive life.

The job of transforming America into an Open Society, peacefully and with justice for all citizens, will require a commitment far beyond any in our history. The first step must be a clear statement of national purpose to tell the world that we are mobilizing all elements of American life. Secondly, there must be public and private programs on an unprecedented scale, aimed at ending poverty and rebuilding urban life. The third step must be a clearly defined timetable tied to these programs: at the end of the first year, so many jobs will have been created, so many new homes built. Part of the reason for the rising frustrations of recent years

**( 1 5 3 )**

was the failure to join announced goals to timetables, so that people could measure performance against promise.

Finally, we must go beyond racism and insure that black people and other minorities get a fair share of the power and responsibility in a democratic society.

All this implies vast social change—in our institutions, in our economy, in our behavior, and even in our thoughts. It won't be easy: yielding privileges and sharing power with the powerless are never painless. But it is necessary if this nation is to fulfill the promise of its past and the dreams of its future.

Building an Open Society will require hard, determined work by all people—white and black. Both suffer under the present system, and both have a stake in transforming it into something decent and humane. I believe deeply that whites and blacks will have to learn to work together. Understandably, there will be frictions, but if we are to survive we must both strive to attain our common goals.

This means that a massive campaign to re-educate Americans will be needed. Fear and mistrust pervade both white and black communities, obstructing joint efforts to make this a decent society, dedicated to diversity. I am confident that it is possible to construct a coalition between black citizens and an enlightened, intelligent white community that acts out of self-interest as well as morality.

White Americans have to be educated to the damage that a racist system does to their own lives. In a world that is three-fourths nonwhite, no white person can be complacent about the oppression black Americans endure. Nor can he be complacent about what is happening to his children: a survey of white schoolchildren in Florida taken after Dr. Martin Luther King, Jr.'s, assassination found that 59 per cent were "elated or indifferent" about it. Even if their parents disliked Dr. King and the civil rights movement, I find it hard to believe that such an expression of hatred from twelve- and thirteen-year-olds doesn't disturb them.

The campaign against racism can't be limited to old clichés about brotherhood; these appeals have been falling on deaf ears for years. It must show that measures taken to benefit black people will benefit all Americans. Much of the resistance to Negro demands is caused by fear that other groups will be ignored or, worse, that white people who cannot afford it will have to foot the bill. Any effort to rebuild our society must take note of the legitimate demands and aspirations of white people, too.

Two out of three poor people are white, and many millions of white families live just above the official poverty line. Lower-middle-class families feel economic pressures and status insecurities that must be dealt with, just as the disproportionate black poverty and deprivation must be dealt with. An Open Society is for everyone—white and black.

Between 1965 and 1968, average weekly wages for production workers rose 13 per cent, but rising taxes and inflation ate up nearly all of the increase. This resulted in anger and frustration. The following bitter monologue by a man in Boston was reported by psychologist Robert Coles:

. . . we're just people, hard-working people, who slave around the clock to pay the bills. I work. My wife works. Let me tell you: when we finish paying our groceries and pay our rent, we're as poor as anyone in America. All we can do is keep our head above water. That's all. And it's a hard fight to do that, to keep ahead of those bills, and the prices that are always going up.

Who cares about us, though? You never hear someone say we

should have it better. If I got sick, we'd all drown. We'd never be able to pay the doctor bills, the way the doctors charge. And my kids, they'll never go to college unless they're smart enough to get a scholarship. But I pick up the papers or turn on the television and all I see is them, them, them: the lousy college students, from rich parents, with their beards and hair and crazy clothes, and their pals, the Negroes. They'll do anything for the Negroes. If you ask me, they enjoy it when the Negroes riot. It excites those college kids, and they shout and scream and attack everyone in the country, except themselves and their buddies, the Negro people on welfare.

This kind of outburst is too often glibly dismissed as backlash or racism, but the problems are real and the emotions are real. There are millions of angry white people leading bleak, joyless lives who vent their frustrations on the better-educated people above them on the status ladder, and the blacks they believe rank below them. What they don't realize is that the programs the civil rights movement is fighting for will benefit them, too. Economic security, universal health insurance, free colleges and better schools are relevant to their needs. If the main emphasis has been on black deprivation, that's because black people as a group suffer most. But these measures are for all Americans, and millions of bitter, alienated people can achieve the security they long for and escape the hatred that consumes them only in an Open Society that restores dignity and decency to *all* citizens.

## COMMUNITY CONTROL

Many Americans—black and white—are alienated from our society because they feel powerless, unable to influence decisions that affect their lives.

Obviously this powerlessness is felt most strongly in the

black ghetto, where decisions are most often made by institutions that are unresponsive to the needs of the people and by individuals who neither live in nor respect the community. Highways and urban renewal projects often destroy black communities, police and welfare departments are often disrespectful to the people they are supposed to be helping, sanitation pickups are few and far between, health facilities and job opportunities are lacking, the schools don't educate the children—and black people have no voice in controlling any of these institutions, which have failed them so completely.

The way to make these institutions responsive to the needs of black people is to decentralize them and encourage effective local control.

Community control is not nearly as revolutionary as it sounds. White suburbanites take for granted their control of local school boards and school budgets. But big-city schools are run by central boards of education, predominately white, which place a low priority on the education of black children. Control of the schools—and of other ghetto institutions—would simply give to the urban poor the same prerogatives enjoyed by the suburban middle class.

It would also fulfill a prime requirement of democracy—maximum citizen participation. As the country has become larger and more complex, more and more power has been vested in centralized bureaucracies, relatively immune from citizen control, and in private corporate structures totally free from any formalized public responsibilities. The creation of new institutions controlled by the citizens whose lives they influence is a step toward the renewal of democratic institutions.

One way to bring government closer to the people and to

improve life in the ghetto is to create elected community councils that would assume responsibility for some governmental functions. Such councils would contract with the city to run the schools, police, and other public agencies in the community, subject to certain uniform guidelines to prevent abuses. A community council might elect to have the city continue to provide these services. Or it might decide that they would function better if they were more responsive to the local community. In that case, the city would transfer funds earmarked for the schools, for example, to the community. The community might then subcontract operation of the schools to a nearby university or teachers' college, or alternatively it might decide to let an elected school board appoint an administrator to run the schools.

Local control is more than just an external "paper" transfer of power; it could bring about tremendous changes. To continue our example of the schools, a central school board might decide that funds for a ghetto district ought to be used to expand gym facilities, in line with a city-wide decision to stress physical education. If the community disagreed, it could put that money instead into new textbooks or into a program of teacher aides. The point is that parents would have a voice in decisions affecting their children, just as white middle-class parents do.

Community councils might set up police-citizen advisory boards to insure adequate police protection. Different communities have different needs, and community control would insure that the ghetto no longer suffered from inadequate services or from decisions, made outside the community, not in the interests of the people in it: a decision, for example, to use more patrol cars when the community's need is foot patrolmen to make the streets safe. Patrolmen responsible to professional police officers appointed by the community would surely be more responsive to the people.

All this would mean not the end of city government, but rather the beginning of effective government. Powers that have been usurped by central bureaucracies and independent agencies would now be exercised by the people themselves through their elected community councils. The city would retain many important functions, not the least of which would be the job of coordinating and overseeing the local councils and funneling power into the communities. It would also have responsibility for city-wide services and agencies.

Effective community control depends on adequate financing. Part of what's wrong with American cities is that they don't have the money to provide necessary services. As middle-class people seek the promised land of suburbia, the tax base shrinks while the need for services by the less-well-off population that remains in the city rises. Yet suburbanites still use urban services—their jobs are often within city limits, as are theatres, museums, zoos, and other public attractions. During their work day they are dependent upon the city's police, sanitation, and hospital services. Their employers depend on markets within the city and on people graduated by city schools. But the suburbanite is not paying for these services, nor is he paying for the full cost of the traffic and other expenses he forces on the city in which he works.

A solution to these urban fiscal problems is creation of a metropolitan taxing authority, which would collect taxes throughout the region, distributing them on a per capita basis to local governments. Some of the money would be funneled by the cities into the local community councils under a formula based on need.

I'm not underestimating the opposition to such major changes, but we have to start from the assumption that the present system has failed, and that unless radical measures are taken to create new structures more responsive to democratic control, America will move even farther away from the ideals it professes. All change is painful, but it will be much more painful to endure the chaos to which the present system is leading us.

Most of the objections to community control I have heard are based on the assumption that black people aren't capable of controlling their own destinies. It's all very reminiscent of Englishmen who claimed their colonies couldn't function without Mother England to control their destiny. Those who seek to perpetuate the colonialism of the ghetto use fancier words, but the meaning is the same.

Many opponents of community control are fearful that "extremists" will take over the ghetto. This ignores the fact that, despite sensational newspaper accounts, "extremists" are a very small part of the total black population. In general, they surface only when it appears that white intransigence is about to crush legitimate black demands. Then they tend to exercise greater influence, capitalizing on the anger within the community.

It is curious, though, that so many people who have tolerated white extremists should suddenly grow fearful at the possibility that black extremists might gain influence. John Birch Society members have been sticking their noses into local school systems and libraries for years, and responsible people have fought them and usually won. Why do some people assume that responsible black citizens will be any less successful? Every poll I've ever seen indicates that black people have little sympathy with the extremists in their midst. Local election results—in Model Cities neighborhood elections, as well as local poverty board elections and polling for state and city representatives—prove this. In fact, when we look at some of the people white districts have sent to Congress or to the State House, there is cause to believe that black people will prove *more* responsible.

The danger of extremist takeover can be met with built-in safeguards. Community councils would derive their power and their funds from the city, state, and federal governments, and abuses of power would be prevented by the accounting procedures and the guidelines these bodies would set. There is no more justification for allowing ghetto communities to abuse their powers in a system of community councils than there is now in allowing communities in the South and elsewhere to ride roughshod over minorities. Community control is not a scheme to get whites out of the ghetto; if anything, it is designed to attract the talents and skills of white people working with the black community. White teachers, policemen, businessmen, and others should all be welcomed, for we need what they can contribute. The only difference is that with community control, their presence will be welcomed by a community that sees them as helpers, not occupiers. It would be senseless for the black community, which has suffered exclusion and the denial of its skills, to turn around and deprive itself of the contributions of others on racial grounds alone.

It has also been charged that community control would perpetuate segregation. But we've never had integration, and so long as black children are denied decent schools, and black families remain imprisoned in rotting tenements and grinding poverty, arguments about integration take on an aspect of unreality. The fact remains that the overwhelming majority of black people live in racial ghettos, and giving them control over their own lives and their own communities may break the cycle of degradation and powerlessness that crushes so many.

This is not a question of "gilding" the ghetto by bettering conditions there. Our aim is twofold: First, to create new mechanisms that will enable people to exercise democratic control over their own neighborhoods and their own lives; and, second, to equip people with the skills, experience, and confidence they need to enter the mainstream of our society.

Community control represents a way to give people a choice. They could decide to move into the dominant society —in fact, the better services and education that would be made available to the ghetto would equip them to make such moves. But at the same time, community control would assure that black people who opted to remain in predominately black neighborhoods would not be forced to pay a penalty in the form of inferior public services and opportunities. Blacks can and, I think, should move into the larger society, but so long as the ghetto exists, its people must be given control over their own lives.

## COMMUNITY DEVELOPMENT

There is another side to community control: economic development for communities that are below average for their region. Some localities have high unemployment or are havens for low-salaried industries. Some, such as big city ghettos or played-out mining areas in Appalachia, have no industry at all and have disproportionate numbers of poor people. While underdeveloped areas can't be isolated from the mainstream and are affected more by national and regional economic policies than by local efforts, it is still important to give communities the additional economic structures and resources to pull themselves up. The ghetto in particular is an economic disaster area, and new ways to build its economy must be found.

In underdeveloped localities, especially in the big cities, community councils should have the power to establish a Neighborhood Development Corporation. The NDCs would have a mandate to undertake job-creating projects within the community. They would lend money to businesses, create cooperatively owned businesses, consumer unions, and housing developments, guarantee private loans to ghetto business, run management-training schools for local businessmen, contract to provide supplies for government operations run by the community, and perform a host of necessary economic functions.

NDCs would be financed through a National Economic Development Bank with regional offices in each of the Federal Reserve districts. The regional office would fund the community groups, provide managerial assistance, and audit their books. It would be financed with government-backed bonds placed through normal financial channels.

The Federal Reserve Board should require member banks to place a certain percentage of their assets in NEDB bonds. This would assure an adequate flow of funds, and at the same time involve federally insured financial institutions in socially responsible use of their assets.

**( 163 )**

This isn't just another scheme for government handouts. It is a financially workable plan that would restore sick urban economies to health. Perhaps the closest analogy to the NEDB is the World Bank. Here is a global institution that finances projects in economically underdeveloped countries. It is recognized that the whole world will benefit from economic aid that reduces the dependency of underdeveloped nations, so the World Bank makes below-market-rate loans, just as the NEDB would funnel money into economically underdeveloped parts of urban America.

Through the locally elected Neighborhood Development Corporation, communities will be able to control their own economies, insofar as possible. People who are now dependent and unskilled would have the pride and dignity of being stockholders in their own community; their shares would be financed through the sale of shares of stock at $2 per share to people in the community and through "sweat equity"—return for work performed.

## NEEDED: A CONCERTED NATIONAL EFFORT

The multitude of programs for poverty and the cities is bewildering even to experts. At the end of 1968 there were about 300 federal programs financed by 400 separate appropriations, administered by 21 federal departments and agencies with 150 bureaus and offices in Washington and 400 regional and field offices.

When responsibility is so diffuse and financing so tenuous, we can only expect failure. The pattern has been for forward-looking legislation to get chopped up in Congressional committees and then passed in watered-down versions. The new programs then have to wait until Congress gets around to passing another bill providing the money, usually far below the authorized amounts. By the time responsibilities are portioned out among the many federal offices, department heads are too busy lobbying for the next year's appropriations to effectively administer this year's programs.

The problem is compounded by the fact that departments that administer poverty and urban programs have other primary constituencies. The Agriculture Department, for example, administers food-stamp programs and a host of others for the rural poor. But the real constituency of the Department is the big farm interests—the large agricultural and packing companies. The Department of Housing and Urban Development is more responsive to big-city mayors than to the ghetto poor. The Labor Department is better equipped to deal with heads of large unions than with the jobless; the Commerce Department is better with business and financial leaders than with small businessmen in the ghetto. The poor have no real voice, no department that speaks to their interests. The exception might have been the Office of Economic Opportunity, but that underfunded agency has been treated like the unwanted stepson of the Establishment. It is obvious that the federal government will have to restructure itself before it can effectively deal with the problems of the poor and the decaying cities they inhabit.

I would favor the appointment of an Executive Vice-President for Domestic Development, charged with administrative responsibility for programs that affect the poor and the cities. He would be the highest-ranking domestic official in the country. Departments dealing with domestic reform programs would report directly to him and he would have budgetary authority and other broad powers to get the job done. Such an official would be able to cut through the tangle of red tape that smothers so many important programs and develop a truly coordinated effort to end poverty. The problems of poverty and urban blight are a seamless weave of bad housing, health, schools, and lack of economic opportunity. They can only be solved by a fully coordinated attack on *all* fronts. The piecemeal approach has produced only chaos.

This new office should also be freed of the budgetary restrictions that hamper present programs. It is impossible to plan effectively or to attract the best staff when nobody knows how much money will be available in the next fiscal year or when the Budget Bureau, which has suddenly emerged as a policy-making rather than an accounting department, might slash appropriations requests.

The Executive Vice-President for Domestic Development should be empowered to devise a five-year or ten-year plan and the whole program should be funded at once. That way, his office would know what funds it would have available for a period long enough to do the job. Provision should be made for supplementary funds to be added when necessary, but no cuts would be allowed once the package passed Congress. The plan should provide for a timetable, with regular progress reports to the nation.

The Executive Vice-President would need expert help in spotting problem areas and devising adequate programs to treat them. The President has a Council of Economic Advisors, which measures the economy and carefully adjusts it to maintain prosperity. It detects the slightest change in prevailing interest rates, money supply, price indexes or industrial production indexes. Just about everything we do is indexed, categorized, filed and recorded. We can't pick up a paycheck or buy a loaf of bread without contributing to one statistical table or another.

But when people were starving in Mississippi, the Agriculture Department didn't know about it. When half the black people in the ghettos were unemployed or underemployed, few people were aware of it. When riots occurred, nobody knew how to explain what happened. Somewhere along the line statistics obscured people, and our view of the social realities of our society became blurred.

What is needed is a Council of Social Advisors, to provide social accounting on a day-to-day basis. It would look for trouble spots around the country, keeping tabs on where the problems are in housing and education, health and recreation, and suggesting action programs to remedy them. It would serve as an early-warning system of social problems.

Such a rational approach to our domestic problems would avoid the costly errors of the past. Only by seeing the problems of the poor and the cities as an interconnected whole can we effectively deal with them. In the past, we built highways leading out of the city, and let mass transit—the lifeline of urban America—die. We gave priority to the space race and let the cities decay. We put programs into the cities and neglected the countryside, so that millions left their rural homes for the cities, intensifying urban problems. We built homes for the middle class in suburbia but ignored decent public housing for the poor. The record of the past has been one step forward and two backward: every positive action has either had negative results or no results at all. It is imperative that we get off this treadmill of failure and start planning and programming in a rational way.

## ECONOMIC SECURITY FOR ALL

Poverty is an abomination that no civilized society with the means to end it can tolerate. The United States is the richest nation in the history of the world, yet nearly 30 million Americans are poor. And that's by the inadequate standards set by federal figures—$3300 for an urban family of four. The government's own estimate of "moderate, but adequate" income is almost three times that figure. The man trying to support a family of four on an income of $3400 would be very surprised to hear that he is not poor.

Who are the poor? They are roughly 30 million of our fellow countrymen. They have the same needs, desires, and aspirations we do. Most are too young or too old to work; nearly half are children and almost a fifth are aged. Three out of four get no public assistance of any kind. A third of the poor live in families headed by a man or woman who worked all year. Seven out of every ten poor people are white. Negroes, who are a tenth of the population, make up three out of ten poor people.

Poverty cuts across racial lines. It crushes millions—black and white. This nation will never be able to hold up its head in the world until it lifts the curse of poverty from every seventh American.

Ending poverty is not solely the concern of "bleeding hearts," liberals, and blacks. It is something that concerns every one of us. The most revered conservative of our times was Ohio Senator Robert A. Taft, who said in 1949: "I believe that the American people feel that with the high production of which we are now capable, there is enough left over to prevent extreme hardship and maintain a minimum standard floor under subsistence, education, medical care and housing, to give to all a minimum standard of decent living and to all children a fair opportunity to get a start in life."

Taking that statement as our starting point, it is clear that twenty years later we have an urgent mandate to devise programs that will end poverty. Simple adjustments in present programs could end poverty for millions.

*The aged.* The five and a half million poor people who are elderly can be helped out of poverty simply by raising social security benefits and by covering *all* people over sixty-two. At present, 10 per cent of the aged are not eligible for social security pensions and the average monthly payment to recipients is only $70—less than half the current poverty standard for individuals. Another 5 million elderly people are just above the admittedly inadequate and arbitrary "poverty line" thanks to their social security checks. Raising the minimum payments to poverty levels would help them too. Payments ought to be adjusted regularly to keep abreast of the cost of living, and social security recipients, like beneficiaries of civil service pensions and private pensions, ought to be allowed to work and to retain their full earnings.

Part of the cost of increasing benefits could be met from general tax revenues, the rest from changes in the regressive social security tax. The present tax is 4.8 per cent on the first $7800, so the poor man pays social security tax on his entire salary, while the president of the company that employs him may only pay the tax on a tenth of his salary. Employers also have to pay an equivalent payroll tax, matching employee contributions, which cuts down on their willingness to hire people for marginal jobs. The tax ought to start at $4000 and cover all income above that figure. This would be more equitable, and also yield enough to make social security a more meaningful national pension plan.

*The working poor.* More than half of all poor people belong to families headed by someone who worked all or part of the year. Dozens of industries don't pay a living wage; their workers, in effect, subsidize the employers through their below-standard wages. California grape-pickers, New York hospital orderlies, Chicago retail clerks, and Memphis sanitation men are among the millions of Americans who put in long, hard hours of work and have little to show for it in their pay envelopes. Many millions more get salaries only slightly above poverty level. In New York City, the highest-cost city in the country, one out of five jobs in the private sector pays less than $80 per week—about what the city welfare department estimates to be its average grant for a family of four.

Millions could be brought out of poverty simply by raising the minimum wage, presently set at $1.60 an hour for most workers, by a dollar to bring it to the $2.60 level. Many employees now covered by lower minimum wage standards— $1.15 for laundry, hotel, hospital workers, and others— should be brought under the national standard. So too, should workers not covered at present: some 12 million, including 8 million who are not even protected by state minimum wage laws. All workers should also be covered by unemployment compensation laws, and benefits should be raised to equal at least half of weekly wages, with additional grants for dependents.

There has been a lot of talk about higher minimum wages causing unemployment, but that hasn't been borne out by recent experience. Actually, as the minimum wage has risen in recent years, unemployment has declined. A big jump in the minimum wage might cause some unemployment, however, especially among teenagers and young people entering the labor market. In order to avoid this the government ought to subsidize the employer who can show that he is unable to continue to do business or to maintain his labor force at the new rates. It is the *employer,* not the worker, who can't meet decent minimum standards, so it is the employer, not the worker, who should be subsidized.

*Guaranteed jobs for all.* At the end of 1968, economists were beaming because the unemployment rate was down to about 3.6 per cent. But two and three-quarter million workers and their families weren't very happy about it—*they* were unemployed. A higher rate considered acceptable by many—say 5 per cent—means more than 4 million jobless. That figure doesn't include many people, especially in the black ghetto, who have lost hope and given up. Because they aren't considered to be actively looking for work, they aren't counted.

Also uncounted are the many millions of people who are working for marginal wages or in jobs far beneath their capabilities, jobs that lead nowhere and have no future. The waste in energy and human potential is appalling. A rational program to put every person who wants to work and is capable of working into a decent job should get top priority. Business must be given the incentives to expand employment, and the government itself must become an employer of last resort.

A good start could be made by federalizing the scandalously inefficient state employment services. A national computerized job-man matching system with federal grants to help workers move to their new job sites would begin to break the log jam of unfilled jobs in one area and high unemployment in another.

Present manpower training programs and on-the-job training programs have demonstrated that private industry is willing to train people if its costs are defrayed. But such programs are still too limited. Subsidies and tax incentives are the usual way government goes about getting business to do things deemed to be in the national interests; they ought to be used for recruiting industry for massive employment and training programs. If an employer buys a machine that will replace some workers, we call it progress and reward him with an accelerated depreciation allowance. Providing jobs for people is "progress" too, and the same incentives to hire and train the jobless should be given.

Since we are asking business to hire marginal workers—the so-called hard-core unemployed—there may be costs to participating companies over and above the training costs. A graduate of an on-the-job training program may be drawing a salary of $100 a week, but for a year or two he may produce at a rate of only $80 a week. The federal government might pick up part of the difference, for a limited time, so that companies will have still more incentives to expand employment.

Inducements in the form of subsidies and tax breaks should be used to encourage industry to build new plants in high unemployment areas such as city ghettos or impoverished rural areas. The ghetto needs a diversified economy, and it is suitable for electronics and computer component plants, as well as other high-technology industries that provide well-paying jobs and can operate efficiently in smaller units in city factories. These industries can benefit from the central location and the labor pool the ghetto offers, and ought to replace the sweatshops and marginal industries that offer, along with retail stores, the ghetto's only jobs. We've already mentioned the role community councils could play, backed by a national development bank. Companies could build plants in the ghetto with loans from the community councils, run the plants and train local residents for jobs and supervisory roles, then turn the plant over to the community after a period of time, perhaps contracting for its output. Tax laws could be modified to provide for accelerated depreciation or even a period of tax exemption, depending on the number of new jobs created.

Other jobs could be created without special inducements or tax incentives. Simply by beginning to tackle this country's enormous environmental problems, we could create enough high-paying jobs to end unemployment. Little has been done to combat pollution, in part because of the great expense. Reconstructing the faulty sewage systems that help poison our rivers would cost many billions of dollars—but it would create half a million jobs, nearly all of them well-paid laborers' jobs. This kind of work helped many Americans climb out of poverty, but such jobs are scarce these days. A federal antipollution program could end black unemployment by reversing the trend that is killing off jobs for the unskilled and uneducated.

But costly antipollution campaigns aren't likely in the near future, and since business is incapable of providing jobs for every American who wants to work, the federal government will have to become the employer of last resort. That is what happened during the depression in the 1930s, when people were paid to rake leaves and shovel air. Anything went, because we recognized that people had to make some kind of minimal income. Today we don't have to have people shoveling air; there is too much unfinished business that needs to be done.

Women now collecting welfare, for example, could be one of our nation's greatest assets. Most of them want to work, but their only skills are housekeeping and child care. Our society doesn't consider these "skills" at all, yet they are vitally important. A nationwide system of comprehensive day-care centers would simultaneously provide jobs for some of these women and free others to enter the labor market. Day-care centers, supervised by trained teachers, could provide preschool education; serviced by doctors and dentists, they could improve the health of children, just as the Head Start program's medical checkups did.

"Unskilled" mothers could be paid to board children who would otherwise grow up in state orphanages or other institutions. In New York, for example, it costs about $7000 a year to keep children in such institutions, while a mother on welfare draws, let's say, $3000. If the city would hire the welfare mother to raise and care for a child in her own home and pay her $5000, she would escape the stigma of welfare, becoming a city employee—a child care specialist, trained and supervised, doing an important job. The child would have a real home, and the taxpayers would save $5000 a year.

New careers can also be created. The demand for professional services has far outstripped the supply of trained professionals. However, professional people now waste valuable time on routine tasks that could just as easily be performed by someone else.

The Urban League has recruited people from the ghetto to work as subprofessional social work aides. Many schools now hire local mothers as teachers' aides. Hospitals need nurses' aides. Private industry has begun to cull out routine tasks from complex engineering jobs and assign them to nonprofessionals. All this has proved that relatively unskilled people can be trained to take over many tasks that were once the sole preserve of the "professional." Nor are these dead-end, meaningless jobs; they are important work and lay the groundwork for future advancement. Many of the Urban League's social work aides have now gone back to school to get social work degrees.

When I served on the Commission on Technology, Automation and Economic Progress, we examined the job-creating potential of subprofessional positions in badly needed areas of public service. Our report, *Technology and the American Economy*, estimates that more than 5 million jobs could be created:

| Source of employment | Job potential (in millions) |
|---|---|
| Medical institutions and health services | 1.2 |
| Educational institutions | 1.1 |
| National beautification | 1.3 |
| Welfare and home care | 0.7 |
| Public protection | 0.35 |
| Urban renewal and sanitation | 0.65 |
| *Total* | 5.3 |

America has enough unfinished business to guarantee a meaningful job to everyone.

*Family allowances.* Even if all the proposals made in the preceding pages are implemented, many families with children—now two thirds of the total poor—will remain below the poverty line. Also, these ideas offer little help to the millions of Americans who make less than the average income—people in the $5000-to-$8000 range. This is where we find the most resistance to black demands for justice. Many working-class and lower-middle-class people lead lives of quiet desperation, hounded by rising prices and economic insecurity. Confronted by great public concern for the poor and subsidized handouts for the rich, they feel left out, angry, and bitter. Their children are denied the decencies of life—regular medical checkups, adequate clothing, and educational opportunities. Together with children from poor families, these youngsters make up half of our nation's children.

They can be helped, and most of the children in poor families can be brought out of poverty, by a system of national family allowances. Every child in America, *as a matter of right,* should receive $40 a month from the government. Payments would be made to their parents, who would be expected to use the money to benefit the children—either directly, through clothing purchases or health checkups, or indirectly, through a higher family standard of living. Administration would be simple: every family with children would register with the Social Security Administration, which would automatically send out checks every month.

Just about every industrialized country in the world—sixty-two nations—make similar payments. Incredible as it seems, such relatively "backward" countries as Iran, Morocco, and Tunisia have had family allowances for years.

That we need expanded aid for children is indisputable. A study of children in Head Start programs found that 70 per cent were receiving their first medical or dental examinations. Nearly half had cavities, and a third had never had smallpox vaccinations. In this affluent country, millions of children have poor diets and are poorly clothed and housed.

Charges that the allowances would be squandered by parents are groundless. Canadians, for example, found that in the first year of their program sales of children's shoes nearly doubled. Family allowances don't lead to a rise in the birth rate, either. People won't have children just to get a measly $40 a month. In fact, France, which has one of the most generous family-allowance schemes, is troubled that its birth rate is too low. It has been proved many times over that when families prosper, they have fewer children.

Even middle-class families faced by high college costs would find family allowances helpful, especially if they were continued past the age of eighteen for children still in school. Canada pegs its allowance to school attendance. This is important, since the majority of children who drop out of school do so for financial reasons.

Some hidebound conservatives might argue that such grants kill the incentive to work. But human nature is such that giving people a little money makes them want more money. Relieving poverty encourages people to work for a better life; hopes are kindled and confidence restored. It is only when hope doesn't exist, when poverty is so complete and devastating, that people give up and lose the will to better themselves.

A universal family allowance program would be costly— it might cost more than $30 billion a year—but since the allowances would be taxable, much of this would be returned to the Treasury. The net cost would be about $20 billion annually—and two thirds of all poor families would no longer be living in poverty.

*Negative income tax.* We have cast a wide net. The aged, the working poor, children, employable adults—all have been covered in some way by the program I've been discussing. But it is not enough; some people will still remain in poverty.

This can be ended by a negative income tax. Under this plan, the government would set a poverty line (hopefully higher than the inadequate $3300 for an urban family of four) and people whose income was below that level would receive payments to bring them up to the standard.

The tax mechanism is an efficient way to distribute this money. Individuals and families could file requests for benefits based on expected below-poverty level income, and then the Internal Revenue's computers could take over, disbursing monthly checks. Provisions would be made for incentives to work—the negative tax allowances would be withdrawn very gradually as individuals become self-supporting.

A negative income tax could be used in tandem with a family allowance plan or it could stand by itself as the mechanism to end poverty for all. It would be a bit cheaper than a family allowance plan, depending on the level of benefits, but it would not help those Americans who are technically out of poverty but whose standard of living is below the average, to the detriment of their children.

Whatever the final form, it is obvious that the nation must have an economic security program that eradicates poverty. We must replace the burdensome welfare system, which destroys initiative, is costly to administer, and provides inadequate income. A family allowance program and a negative income tax both fill the bill, and they have an added advantage: they avoid degrading means tests. At present, poor people have to go, hat in hand, to ask for charity. That's why only one in four get help. The stigma attached to welfare is designed to discourage people from claiming what should be, in a civilized, affluent, society, a matter of right.

Our economic security program assumes that everyone should have an income floor beneath which he will not be allowed to fall; that such a minimum should be high enough to assure a decent standard of living; and that this is a *right* to which people are entitled.

## PAYING FOR ECONOMIC SECURITY

The economic security program I am proposing is not cheap. In the following pages, there will be other proposals —for decent housing, health care, and education for all— that are also expensive. An Open Society can't be built on the cheap. We've already seen what happens when we declare "war" on poverty and then try to achieve meaningful results with inadequate funds.

Where will the money come from? The first place to look for added funds is in present programs that should be cut because they aren't as important as domestic reconstruction. About $5 billion in subsidies to corporations and individuals amounts to a raid on the national Treasury. They could painlessly, and with justice, be diverted to economic security programs. So too could some of the money now spent on space races, supersonic transports, and highways. Highway-use taxes, by law, are placed in a special trust fund that can only be used to build more highways; this amounts to about $5 billion. We've seen what excessive road-building has done to mass transit and to cities; these funds should be transferred to general revenues. It's more important to build houses for people to live in than to build roads for cars to drive on.

The greatest source of funds would be the natural increase in federal revenues. If the economy continues to grow at the relatively high rate of recent years, federal revenues at the present tax rates *will increase by $15 billion to $16 billion a year*. And this will be more than doubled with the end of expenditures on the Vietnam war; within two or three years after the end of the war, an additional $20 billion to $30 billion annually would be freed.

More money could be raised by reforming our inequitable tax system. Unbelievable though it may be, poor people pay taxes—estimates range from $300 million to $1 billion a year—driving them deeper into poverty. People in the $4000 to $5000 bracket pay a higher percentage of their incomes in federal and local taxes than any other group. While the poor and less well-off are bled, the rich are blessed with a wide variety of loopholes. In 1967, 367 individuals with incomes of over $100,000 paid no income tax at all, while oil companies, taking advantage of the 27½ per cent depletion allowance, paid a tax of only 8.8 per cent of net income. (Individuals in the lowest income brackets paid at a rate of 14 per cent.)

Experts have estimated that tax reform could eliminate loopholes by granting all taxpayers a standard deduction of 5 per cent of gross income and limiting itemized deductions only to amounts exceeding that figure, as well as reducing favorable treatment for capital gains and speculative income. They claim that tax rates could then be reduced. Nearly all taxpayers would be paying lower taxes, but revenues would increase by over $7 billion.

Assuming that welfare payments were replaced by the negative income tax, still another $5 billion a year, at the least, would be freed. Some of the present welfare costs would continue, since caseworkers are badly needed to help people overcome their special problems, but the bulk of present welfare expenditures could be diverted into more effective assistance programs.

All of these steps free a sum that is in the neighborhood of $60 billion a year to be used as an investment in America's future. And it should be seen as an investment, not as an expense.

Putting people in jobs, giving people incentive to better their lot, putting shoes on kids' feet and books in their hands are self-liquidating investments—they pay for themselves.

The GI Bill is a perfect example of how social programs return more than they cost. About $14.5 billion has been spent to finance the GI bills; 7.8 million people obtained specialized training under the programs, including 2.2 million who are college-educated. Every year they pay a billion dollars in taxes; over their working lives they will pay far more than the cost of the help they got to finance their education.

We've had the same experience in current poverty programs. A typical on-the-job trainee returns his training costs in taxes within two years. Job Corps graduates, even if they never make much more than the minimum wage, will pay taxes totaling double their training costs. It costs five times more to maintain a man in prison than it does to keep him in school.

Increasingly it becomes clear that the question is not "Can we afford it?" but "Can we afford *not* to end poverty and deprivation?"

## IMPROVED HEALTH SERVICES

Few people realize how closely adequate health care is tied to employment. Job training programs have found that one of the biggest reasons people don't stay with newly found jobs is poor health. It is also the biggest reason for voluntary retirement and for not working among men in their prime working years. Regular medical checkups are unheard of among the poor and lower-income groups because of the cost, and even middle-class families find it hard to meet medical bills. And medical costs are soaring. Hospital rates are rapidly advancing to the $70-per-day level, and drug prices are unreasonably high. Most families still have no medical insurance and few with incomes under $5000 have adequate hospital insurance. A serious illness can drive these families to the wall.

The Medicare program was established to help the aged meet their high health costs. For a modest insurance fee, people over sixty-five could get free medical attention. The program works. Many lives have been saved and hundreds of thousands of elderly people can now afford to get decent medical treatment in dignity *as a matter of right.*

But why only the elderly? Medicare grew out of a twenty-year battle to establish a universal health system. Since we Americans always seem to tackle social problems in piecemeal fashion, such a system was set up for only one group in our population—the elderly. It is time we extended it to the entire population. It makes no sense to assure decent health care to one person just because he is sixty-five and not to another, not even to a child, whose chance for a long, productive life may depend on medical treatment now. I don't think it is an accident that America lags behind other countries in key health indicators such as infant and maternal mortality rates, and is also without the universal health plan that other countries have.

A universal health plan, financed by a modest insurance or prepayment system, should be established to provide a guaranteed minimum standard of medical care. At the same time, community councils in poverty or low-health neighborhoods should be given health grants to establish visiting health services and accessible, community-controlled clinics.

## A NATIONAL HOUSING PROGRAM

We can't become an Open Society so long as the poor and the black are segregated into rotting slums, without the housing choices available to better-off Americans. Decent housing isn't something that belongs only to the rich or to white people. Top priority should be given to establishing every family's *right* to a decent home.

America will have to build at least 27 million new or rehabilitated housing units over the next ten years to replace substandard homes and to meet the increased needs of a growing population. Subsidized housing for low- and moderate-income families will have to account for much of this—at least 800,000 units a year, equal to the total number of public housing units built since 1934. Assuring a decent home for all families will take more than federal building programs; it will also take effective steps to desegregate housing and the creation of a national housing industry.

*Integration.* Because they have few choices, black people pay more and get less for their housing dollar. One way to create choices is to strictly enforce and extend the Open Housing Law. Stiff fines, swift compliance procedures, giving victims of discrimination the right to sue for damages: these simple steps would go a long way toward solving the problem. I'd also favor federal laws to permit cities to build public housing in the suburbs, where zoning laws are now used to preserve one-race, one-class towns. These would be small units—no high-rise buildings—that would preserve the character of the area.

Perhaps the fastest way to get a better racial balance between city and suburb is through rental or subsidized sale to blacks of houses repossessed by the Federal Housing Administration, now often put on the market through realtors who sell to whites only. The FHA and other agencies which insure loans and mortgages should be barred from dealing with any broker or owner of rental property who discriminates.

Racial balance through tax incentives is another interesting proposal. Reporter Ben H. Bagdikian summarized it this way:

A city may have 40 percent Negroes downtown, but its whole metropolitan area may contain only 12 percent Negroes. Every buyer and seller of a house who acts to move toward the 12 percent ratio of Negroes would get a special benefit, in a tax forgiveness for the seller and an advantageous FHA mortgage rate for the buyer. The same would be true of those involved in transferring property to whites in areas that are more than 12 percent Negro. After the 12 percent Negro proportion was reached in any individual suburb, the special benefit would stop, inhibiting wholesale drift toward all-Negro or all-white buying.

*Taking the profits out of slums.* Local housing codes are a patchwork of antiquated and inefficient regulations. The Department of Housing and Urban Development should establish a uniform code that would set minimum standards for safe and decent dwellings. Then owners of substandard buildings should be refused federally insured loans and depreciation for the buildings on their taxes, while owners who made improvements and met the standard got extra depreciation benefits. Cities could supplement this by stiffer fines and even prison sentences for landlords who violate the housing laws. At present, an owner can get away with a $25 fine, hardly a deterrent.

Decent buildings in the ghetto often deteriorate because their owners can't get insurance coverage, and banks won't make improvement loans or give mortgages on uninsured property. The federal government ought to back a pool of insurance companies to provide coverage for such buildings. Insurance pools now provide auto insurance to drivers considered greater than average risks; housing needs the same break.

There will still be some owners who can't or won't bring their buildings up to standard. These should be taken over by the city and turned over to the local community council to be rehabilitated and turned into tenant cooperatives, with federal aid.

*Creating a national housing industry.* Any plan to build as many as 27 million housing units in ten years has an Alice-in-Wonderland quality about it, for the housing "industry" is a jumble of thousands of contractors, construction companies, and developers. Annual construction rates limp along at less than 1.5 million units a year, mostly suburban one-family homes or speculative luxury urban developments.

It will take a National Housing Corporation, jointly owned by the federal government and private industry, to mass-produce housing the way we do cars. The first task will be to develop new technology. The laggard construction industry now spends two tenths of 1 per cent of its revenues on research and development; a typical growth industry spends 1.5 per cent.

Unions are often blamed for obstructing development of new materials, just as they are blamed for keeping black workers out of construction jobs. The creation of a national housing industry that would double the production of homes, would provide real job security for this highly seasonal industry, and create so many new jobs that unions would find it in their own interest to desegregate and to welcome new techniques and materials.

There is no reason why we can't "build" homes in factories. Some of this has already been done on a small scale. Modular units can be built in one piece and installed at the building site. New materials can be developed; wonders are being done with cement and plastics. A mass volume market would result in the technological breakthroughs needed to bring prices down without lowering standards. After all, when the supersonic airplane was being planned metals strong enough to fly at such speeds didn't exist. Because they were needed, and because there was a market for them and funds available to develop them, the required metals were developed and produced in the necessary quantity.

Order can't come out of chaos unless stable economic conditions prevail. When "tight money" became official policy in 1967, new housing trailed off to its lowest point since World War II. A 1 per cent rise in the interest rate (the cost of borrowing money for mortgages) adds 10 per cent to the cost of a project. For a national housing policy to work, lower interest rates will have to be maintained.

The federal government should also use tax concessions and loan guarantees to attract private financial backing, and the FHA must relax its loan restrictions to take social benefits into account. Federal revenues alone can't rebuild our cities; concessions will have to be made to get private industry to back a national homebuilding program.

*Model cities.* Rebuilding slums takes more than bricks and mortar; it also takes a co-ordinated attack on the problems that breed slums, and it takes participation by the people who live there. The Model Cities program is the most imaginative federal urban program in memory, and is firmly based on community participation. But the initial planning grants to sixty cities totaled less than the cost of planning New York's Pan Am Building. If that's the kind of money that will be made available, Model Cities, like so many programs before it, will wither away and die, leaving behind it a trail of broken promises and angry resentment.

*New towns.* It won't be enough to rebuild cities. We've

also got to build new ones. It's been done before, in an un-
planned, chaotic way. Huntsville, Alabama, was a sleepy
country town until NASA put its space installation there.
Now it's a thriving city of 150,000. Oak Ridge, Tennessee,
was made possible by atomic energy facilities. Washington is an
example of a city created by government.

But there is a new kind of city that could be built—New
Towns—built from scratch. Industries could be brought in
so that the town won't deteriorate into a bedroom suburb of
the nearest big city. A whole range of houses and jobs at all
levels would insure that all income groups will live there.

A fundamental part of any national housing plan should
be the creation of 100 New Towns with populations of no
less than 100,000 people in each. They should have industries and office complexes to provide employment, and
should be located far enough away from present metropolitan regions so that they would not be absorbed into old patterns. The New Towns could be financed by federal revenues, federally backed bonds in the regular bond market,
and private investment. It might be necessary to provide incentives for private industry, but I doubt it. Some large companies are already considering building new cities. The
enormous market that would be created would be incentive enough. People could be encouraged to move to the
New Towns through moving subsidies and the promise of
jobs.

It is doubtful if meaningful integration can be accom-
plished within the next ten years in many of our metropolitan areas, where half of the city-dwellers are black and 95
per cent of the suburbanites are white. But New Towns offer
the chance to create totally integrated communities, and at

the same time to relieve the problems of slums and congestion in our present cities. New Towns located in the South could stem the flight of emigrants from the countryside and also close the prosperity gap between the South and other regions.

*Public housing.* Some drastic changes have to be made in our approach to public housing. It is better—and cheaper —to subsidize rents for low-income tenants than to build vast housing projects that quickly become vertical slums. A step in this direction was made through the rent supplement program, but it is underfunded, smothered by restrictions, and is in effect limited to ghetto areas.

Federal funds should be made available to public housing authorities to rent apartments in buildings that meet the standard code requirements. In addition, rent certificates could be issued directly to families who qualify for public housing, enabling them to buy it on the open market. In each case, the government would make up the difference between the market rental and what each family could afford. Owners of all larger apartment buildings could be required to rent a percentage of their units to the housing authority as they became vacant; in new structures built with federal loan guarantees, apartments could be set aside for the program from the beginning.

Such programs, together with FHA repossession sales to families who qualify for public housing, construction of small public housing units in suburban areas, and scattering sites throughout all parts of cities would assure economic and racial integration.

The government will also have to build apartment projects; there is no other way to meet the immense demand for adequate housing. But instead of segregating the poor in high-rise developments, such projects should be open to all. Well-off tenants could be charged market rentals which would help pay building costs, while public housing tenants paid lower rates. No one need know who is being subsidized, removing the housing equivalent of the means test. If such projects proved economically viable, they might be run by a consortium of private investors and housing authorities or community councils.

In ghetto areas, a community council might decide to build new housing for the poor. The Public Housing Authority could construct the buildings and then turn them over to the council to run, together with the funds to pay operating costs and stipends for the social services the poor need but do not get in today's housing projects. The turnkey method—designed to cut red tape—should be encouraged, too. In turnkey projects, housing authorities contract with private developers to build homes on a cost-plus basis. The authority promises to buy the project when it has been built, and sometimes hires the developer to manage it. About a third of all public housing units started in 1968 were in turnkey projects.

Home ownership for moderate-income families should also be encouraged, through federally insured below-market-rate mortgages at longer-than-usual terms. Labor—called "sweat equity"—might be used as part of the down payment. A man could work on the construction of his own home, contributing his labor as a down payment on the house. The value of his work would be deducted from the cost of the house, and federally insured, long-term mortgages would cover the rest of financing. There is no reason why this shouldn't also apply to small apartment houses. A social dividend here is that the individual gains job experience and is helped to qualify for a new career in construction work.


## EDUCATION

*The urban grant university.* Back in 1862, in the midst of the Civil War, Congress passed the Morrill Act, which donated 17 million acres of federal land to the states to create colleges "for the benefit of agriculture and the mechanic arts . . . in order to promote the liberal and practical education of the industrial classes." These land-grant colleges, now flourishing state universities, were the backbone of American higher education. They enabled millions to go to college, and provided agricultural research and other services for our then-rural economy.

Our nation now needs a similar system of urban grant universities. Colleges now in the cities have failed the urban population. Many of them only make contact with the ghetto surrounding them in the process of "urban-renewing" part of it out of existence, packing the slums tighter with people evicted from their homes by the university's bulldozer.

Urban grant universities should be established in every city of 200,000 or more, not only to provide a first-class education, but also to serve the urban communities just as their predecessors served farm communities. They could be a prime resource for community councils, helping to plan community projects, contracting to run schools and hospitals, and providing experts in housing and other areas. They could conduct adult education programs and train people for new careers as semiprofessional aides.

Tuition should be free. Any high school graduate who met course requirements would be admitted, and remedial training would be provided to bring victims of our inadequate inner-city public schools up to college-entrance levels.

College costs are climbing steeply, and there are not enough classroom openings. Despite all the misleading talk about the availability of scholarships, we have set up an income barrier that keeps people from going as far as their potential and skills will permit. This represents an incredible waste of human resources. Some countries not only provide free education right through to postgraduate studies, but they also pay students' living expenses. At the very least, we should establish the principle of the right to free higher education for all who want it and have the ability.

*Integrating the schools.* Few issues arouse so much emotion as bringing white and black children together in the public schools. Many white parents in the North were all in favor of school desegregation when they saw television films of parents in Little Rock and New Orleans screaming obscenities at six-year-old black children. But when it came to their own kids' schools, which were just as segregated as those in the South, many of the same people suddenly found that they were concerned about preserving the (all-white) "neighborhood school." The parents who boasted of riding miles to school in their youth, and who now bus their kids clear across town to private schools, are often the people who wail the loudest about busing public school children.

But school integration is vital for all children—white and black. It is important for the black child because, so long as ghetto schools remain inferior institutions, his best hope for a quality education lies in attending the predominately white schools that now get the best teachers, books, and equipment. White children, on the other hand, are in danger of growing up in an educational hothouse, unprepared for the real world. As the former head of the Darien, Connecticut, school system, Dr. Gregory C. Coffin, stated when he resigned that post, ". . . because of their money and their position, these kids will probably be leaders, and they're being prepared for that role with only a wildly unrealistic view of life."

As the more affluent whites move to the suburbs or send their children to private schools, urban school systems become blacker. Black children are already in the majority in the public schools of Chicago, Detroit, Pittsburgh, St. Louis, and other cities; they comprise 95 per cent of Washington, D.C.'s, school population.

Whatever the reason for it—urban housing patterns or Southern defiance—school segregation is illegal and an intolerable obstacle to an Open Society. Strict enforcement of the law has been hampered by Congressional pressures and inadequate funds for investigation and enforcement officers. Also, the main threat in the enforcement arsenal—cutting off federal funds—is like the atom bomb: too damaging to all concerned to be of tactical use. When Southern states barred black citizens from voting, the government sent in federal registrars, who took over the job of registering voters. This precedent could be followed in enforcing desegregation. When a school district breaks the law by ignoring court desegregation orders, the federal government should be empowered to dismiss the lawbreakers, replacing them with a new board of qualified local citizens pledged to carry out the law.

Busing, pairing of schools, and other feasible techniques should be used to encourage integration. And suburban schools shouldn't be exempt. Incentives could be offered to suburban districts to accept inner-city children or to arrange for pupil exchanges. Even without such incentives, Hartford's suburban schools accepted 800 black children from the city; similar programs elsewhere have proved successful.

Perhaps the most promising technique for achieving educational excellence as well as integration is the educational park. An educational park is a complex that clusters several schools, of all levels, in one central location. Like an advanced medical center, its very size means it can afford expensive teaching tools and facilities that would be out of reach for a single school. Because it draws its pupils from a wide area of the city, it breaks down neighborhood racial barriers. Federal grants could be provided to induce cities to build these better schools, just as such grants are available to cities to build highways.

*Improving the public schools.* Integration is no panacea. Children—black and white—are not getting the quality education this country is capable of providing. Even the "good" schools are more concerned with programming children to pass tests than they are with fostering human values. The public schools could be rehabilitated with more money, more parent participation, and better teaching.

City schools are strapped for money. Voters, bristling under high taxes, can be counted on to kill school bond issues. Federal money clearly has to be put into local school systems. The Office of Education should declare a minimum level of per-pupil spending, and then make up the difference between that level and what local communities can afford to pay for schools. A minimum local school tax rate should be set to prevent localities from simply shifting their responsibilities onto Washington. In addition to providing more funds, this would equalize pupil expenditures between suburban systems that spend $1500 per pupil and ghetto schools that spend $500. Bonus allotments should be made available to low-achievement school districts for reading specialists, teaching machines, or other needed programs that would bring them up to standard. Ghetto schools, especially, have to be saturated with special services to overcome the handicaps of the slum environment.

But this money would be wasted if it were simply funneled through the present incompetent bureaucracies that have made the public schools a sanctuary for security-minded people who don't care about developing their students' potentials. The schools might as well shut up shop if their administrators don't agree to share control with concerned parents. As the Bundy Report on New York City school decentralization stated, "There is an intimate relation between the community and the ability of public education to function effectively . . . [if] the community regards the school as an agency in which they have an investment, which acknowledges a responsibility for pupil achievement—in short, as their own—children will enter the school with positive expectations."

This implies a drastic shift in power. School administrators, teachers, and unions will have to surrender a part of their power to parents. Their refusal to do this nearly wrecked New York City in 1968, when the teachers' union called three strikes that demanded elimination of effective decentralization of the schools. Its intentions were clouded by charges of violation of due process, harassment, and anti-Semitism, but the real issue was power. The teachers (or at least the ones who struck—a large minority broke into the schools to teach their pupils) were backed by supervisors and principals fearful that schools controlled by the community wouldn't stick to the old civil service promotion lists in hiring supervisory staff.

Decentralization may represent a threat to the present holders of power, but it represents the hope of a new day for children, parents, and teachers. I visited the embattled Ocean Hill-Brownsville school district that was the focal point of the New York strikes. This experimental district was sabotaged from the beginning by forces that wanted it to fail, and it was beset by public controversy. Racial "militants" seeking a confrontation with the police and the striking teachers added to the district's problems. The ability of the teachers and administrators to keep these self-proclaimed "leaders" from speaking for them and for the community, as well as what I observed in the schools, confirmed my faith in the concept of community control.

Youngsters were learning as never before. They were reading and learning math and making progress that was unheard of under the old system. They were being taught black history and black culture—but they also got lessons on the meaning of Rosh Hashanah and other Jewish holidays, as well as in the customs of other peoples. They were being educated for an Open Society by a young teaching staff that was eager to work in the district. One teacher told me that he could never again teach under the old system, which made teachers afraid to try something new: "We aren't required to serve the system here—just the kids." Another teacher told me how important it was to her to have the help of concerned parents, and parents told me how important the schools had become to the whole community since the experiment began. For the first time, many parents were involved in the schools and participated in their children's education. The schools I saw were no longer the usual ghetto failure factories—they were schools that met the needs of the children, fulfilled the hopes of their parents, and gave their teachers a strong new joy in their work.

Even with additional funds and parent participation, public education will fail unless it attracts dedicated teachers like the ones I met in Ocean Hill-Brownsville. As Kenneth Clark has said, "A normal child who is expected to learn, *who is taught* and who is required to learn will learn."

The teaching profession ought to have the recognition it deserves. The present system of lumping all teachers together—the effective with the ineffective—paying them the same salary, and subjecting them to the same restrictions doesn't make sense. Neither does the licensing system, which assumes that accumulating a certain number of credits in educational theory makes a person qualified to teach a child in the ghetto.

I'd like to see a system of teaching internships. Before a teacher could qualify for a full-fledged position, he should teach under the supervision of a master teacher. Creation of the higher-paid post of master teacher would recognize merit and accomplishment in teaching, just as superior accomplishment is rewarded in other fields. Interns could be recruited from Peace Corps returnees, VISTA volunteers, and others who may not meet present license requirements but who exhibit the compassion and the zeal so noticeably lacking in our schools.

The very best teachers ought to be in the ghetto schools, and, as specialists performing the most exacting and demanding work, they should get the rewards due them. Sending inexperienced or unsympathetic teachers into ghetto schools is too much like having interns perform complex heart operations, while the specialists treat healthy people for common colds. If we staffed the schools of the ghetto with master teachers and made these schools accountable to the community we would transform the dying institution of public education.

## THE POLICE AND THE COMMUNITY

The ghetto distrusts the police, and the police fear the ghetto. This situation is especially tragic because the ghetto, a high-crime area, desperately needs police protection. But so long as black people see the police as the oppressive, intruding arm of White America, the conflict will surely deepen.

More black policemen are essential, especially higher-ranking officers in command positions. However, more basic ways must also be found to make the police accountable to the community. For a time it seemed as if civilian review boards were the answer. A few cities established such boards, made up of prominent citizens and, occasionally, police representatives, to handle citizen complaints against policemen. But when New York, a liberal stronghold, rejected its review board by a two-to-one vote in a 1967 referendum, it became obvious that such panels would be difficult if not impossible to establish.

New York policemen's association waged a campaign of misrepresentation and fear to defeat the board. But they had one valid point. "Why pick on us?" they asked. "Other public institutions sometimes abuse people and aren't subject to citizen review." As government bureaucracies take on a life of their own, removed from accountability to the public, some individuals do abuse their authority. I think we would do well, following the example of Sweden and some other countries, to create the position of *ombudsman*—a public protector whose job is to investigate and publicize citizen complaints against public officials. The ombudsman has the power to issue summonses, subpoena documents, and conduct open hearings. His recommendations, because of the prestige of the office and the publicity he commands, are hard for officials to ignore.

Direct community control of public institutions, including the police, would also serve to reduce friction. Day-to-day operations of the police force would remain in the hands of professional police administrators, just as community-controlled schools would be run by professional educators. But with control—of funds, supplies, hiring, etc.—vested in elected representatives of the community, and subject to city-wide standards, the police would be directly accountable to the public, rather than to an inbred self-protective bureaucracy. Some police tasks, such as narcotics bureaus, detective squads, and similar specialized duties, would continue to be performed by a central police department, but the order-keeping functions of the police would be best performed by local precincts serving their communities. With safeguards to prevent possible abuses, such locally controlled precincts would increase trust and thus insure the greater cooperation of the local community in the preservation of order.

Such community control is already in operation in wealthy suburbs. James Q. Wilson reports, in his *Varieties of Police Behavior,* that officials of a wealthy suburban Long Island village informed the county police department that "They wanted to be sure they had as policemen, men who understood the special problems of a rich community." They were assured they'd get "well-screened men who would understand their special needs." The ghetto too, needs men who understand its special needs and are responsive to the people who live there.

At the same time, we must raise police standards. The bulk of America's policemen are underpaid and undertrained. Higher salaries, regional police training academies, better testing procedures, and extended periods of internship are needed to make police work more professional. A basic goal of this training, especially for policemen in the cities, must be to educate the racism out of recruits.

Some towns in California, as part of their training programs, give new policemen $5 and send them out of town to spend a week on Skid Row so they can get the feel of what it's like to be at the bottom. They also order recruits to get themselves locked up for a night in the "drunk-tank" in a nearby town so they will know how it feels to be a prisoner. One young policeman, indescribably depressed by the experience, told a reporter what a lift it gave him when one of the jailers addressed him as "Mister." This is one recruit who isn't likely to call grown men "Boy" when he gets his badge and uniform.

Ultimately, however, the way to reduce crime is to end the conditions that cause it. Assault, robbery, burglary— crimes against individuals and their property—are the direct result of poverty and slum housing, and the anger they fire. We can put ten cops on every corner and staff our courts with hanging judges and these crimes will continue, so long as the conditions that foster them persist.

Many of the proposals I have discussed are practical ones, which could be implemented tomorrow if America really wanted to use its resources in a rational manner to create an Open Society. Others may seem utopian in an era which seems at times inclined more to repression than to renewal. The goal of all of these proposals is to make ours an egalitarian society, one in which people of all races and backgrounds have control over their lives.

Control is really the name of the game today. There was a time when handouts of one sort or another were considered the way to deal with social problems. It is increasingly clear now that black people and other minorities resent it when the great white father comes bearing gifts, demanding complete subservience in return. The real question today is not whether White America will yield some extra goodies, but whether it will move over and allow black people to share some of its power and some of its privileges.

# CHAPTER FOUR

# RESPONSIBILITY FOR CHANGE

No American—white or black—can escape the consequence of the continuing social and economic decay of our major cities.

From every American . . . new attitudes, new understanding, and, above all, new will.

—REPORT OF THE NATIONAL ADVISORY COMMISSION ON CIVIL DISORDERS

R ACE RELATIONS and the problems of the cities directly affect every area of American life and every American citizen, white or black. It is no longer possible for anyone to sit back and watch television films of protests and marches as if civil rights were some kind of spectator sport, and to say with complacent helplessness: "Yes, but what can I—one lone human being—do?" We will not have progress until the thousands of lone human beings who make the decisions for the private sector decide to bring the money, managerial skills, and jobs at their disposal to bear on the problems of poverty and race relations. Nothing will change until millions of white Americans, in the loneliness of their own consciences, face the truth about this country and begin to change their attitudes, from the inside out. The Open Society will be just one more treacherous dream until millions of black Americans organize themselves to seize the opportunities that are already there and win the opportunities that aren't.

## THE PRIVATE SECTOR

Business has a stake in the cities. Corporate headquarters alone, located in the ten largest cities, represent a capital investment of nearly $100 billion dollars. Urban America provides the employees, the resources, and the markets for business. The business community has to be aware of what the consequences will be if the cities upon which it depends go on becoming poorer and blacker. History teaches that when an aggrieved and suppressed minority takes over politically, it often does so with its most irresponsible people. America has been lucky that the first black mayors of major cities have been men of the stature of Carl Stokes of Cleveland and Richard Hatcher of G..y, but only time will tell if these men will be the exception or the rule. The business community, especially, knows that its survival is tied to the development of a responsible black electorate that shares equally in the rewards and responsibility of our society. In this context, *profit* takes on a new meaning for enlightened businessmen, who know that unless today's profits are in part used for important social ends, there may not be any profits tomorrow. Henry Ford II has put it: "There is no longer anything to reconcile—if there ever was—between the social conscience and the profit motive. . . . It seems clear to me that improving the quality of society—investing in better employees and customers for tomorrow—is nothing more than another step in the evolutionary process of taking a far-sighted view of return on investment."

Many corporations are now willing to become involved in social problems and to step up hiring of black workers. Some do so for "fire insurance"—they don't want to be hit by riots. Some want a bigger share of the Negro market—$30 billion and growing fast. Some know that the only way they can attract the bright college graduates who will be their future managers is to give them a chance to participate in social change. For many others, it is purely a moral question: they cannot reconcile wealth in the midst of poverty and injustice.

Whatever the reason, the business community is beginning to accept the responsibilities that go with its power and status. There is now a new breed of businessman, far more sophisticated and enlightened, committed to using his talents and resources to rebuild our torn society.

Even with this newfound concern, however, business' involvement in social issues is not on a scale commensurate with its enormous stake in their solution. Too often, the reason for this is not the lack of will or even a failure to understand the depth of the problem; it is simply not knowing what to do.

The obvious place to start is in hiring and personnel practices. HIRE NEGROES should replace the traditional THINK signs in executive offices. It should be the credo of every personnel department that spent such time and energy in *not* hiring black workers in the past. Hire Negroes—not just the Phi Beta Kappa from the Harvard Business School, and not just the beautiful secretary who looks like Lena Horne. Hire dumb Negroes; hire mediocre Negroes. I run into dumb white people and mediocre white people every day; they have jobs, sometimes pretty good ones. There is no reason why average and below-average Negroes shouldn't have jobs too. So long as a company is just looking for a couple of not-too-black "Exhibit A's," it's not being serious about changing its hiring policies—and it isn't fooling anybody either. If every large employer in the country were to hire two new black workers for every hundred men it now employs —whether it "needed" these new men or not—the burden would be small for each company, and they would end unemployment while coming closer to the goal of a racially balanced work force.

One way to establish fair hiring procedures is to scrap

those prejudicial tests that don't really measure anything of value. Companies should stick to job-related tests that score for potential and desire to learn, and they need to be sensitive to the fears and doubts of minority workers for whom the interviewing and testing procedure is so often a terrifying experience. Black applicants could be given a handicap, like the one veterans get on civil service exams, to make up for the opportunities they never had. This is another realistic way to bring a company's work force into better racial balance.

Another way to find more black employees is to break down the credentials fixation that so many companies have. The janitor of yesterday, who had little schooling and was often illiterate, is today's custodial engineer, required to have a high school diploma and pass a battery of tests. The job hasn't changed, but the complex paperwork required to hire and qualify the applicant has.

Job tasks can be broken down, too. The elements of a job that require special skills can be assigned to trained workmen, leaving the more routine duties for unskilled personnel to do. In this way, skilled workers are more productive and new jobs at entry levels are created. Business did this during World War II, when there was a labor shortage; it can do it again. The new jobs could also serve as apprenticeship positions for future upgrading to skilled levels.

Another lesson we learned from the war experience was that accelerated training programs can teach complex jobs to almost anyone who is motivated. When I was in Vietnam, I saw GIs operating fantastically complex equipment that cost many thousands of dollars—advanced electronic and radar equipment that most companies wouldn't entrust to anyone who didn't have his MIT degree tattooed on his fore-head. I asked these men where they got their skills. "In the Army," they said. A month or two at special Army schools was enough. When I asked them about their backgrounds, I found that none had more than a high school degree and many were dropouts. Any businessman who says that men with poor schooling can't handle complex jobs is confessing that the wonders of private enterprise, about which we hear so much, can't match the results obtained by a government department.

Many companies do have successful training programs. They take advantage of federal on-the-job training aid, or expand their own ongoing programs, and the Urban League and other community organizations help them find and train applicants. In a few companies, training programs are placed in the hands of the most imaginative executives, who have gone far beyond teaching routine job skills. They've set up basic education courses to improve reading skills, con-sumer education programs to help trainees use their pay-checks more effectively and avoid loan sharks, and special services such as company-run day care centers for working mothers.

A company's sincerity can be measured by the numbers of black supervisors and executives it hires. Simply opening up jobs is not enough. Unless black people are given a share of corporate power and influence and are placed in positions *above* as well as *below* white people, "equal opportunity" will have a hollow sound and a bitter taste.

Businesses that cry about the lack of trained Negroes for supervisory jobs probably haven't looked at the talent in their own workforce. One executive, in desperation, studied the personnel records of Negro employees. He found college graduates sweeping floors and bright young men stuck in dead-end jobs. A crash training course was set up and a company-wide program of upgrading employees was successfully established.

The key to all successful hiring programs is the involvement of top corporate officials. I recall meeting one company president who told me that he had signed the Plans for Progress pledge in 1963 and then simply assumed that his plant managers and personnel people would comply with the memorandum he sent out. He didn't even think about it for a couple of years, until he learned one day that his company was being threatened with a suit charging discriminatory hiring. I managed to keep from asking him about his eyesight —surely he must have noticed that there were no more Negro employees in his office than there were before his high-sounding memorandum went out. Anyway, the legal action shook him up. He called a top-level staff meeting and informed his department heads that he wanted to see progress reports on their hiring of Negro workers, and that he expected every plant to have roughly the same proportion of blacks as were in that city's labor force. Then, as he walked out the door, he looked back and said that henceforth all executive promotions and raises would be judged on a number of performance standards, and fulfilling minority hiring policies was at the top of the list. "One thing I found out from that experience," he said. "If the top man doesn't lay down the law, no action will be taken."

Of course, this man was something of an exception; many executives don't want to rock the boat. They're afraid of public reaction, the board of directors, or the stockholders, although studies show that social action doesn't run into strong objections from any of these groups.

To get weak-sister executives off the hook and to help business get involved in more than just hiring actions, industry-wide committees ought to be formed, to mobilize companies and serve as the social-action arm of the industry. Individual companies could—and should—still run separate programs of their own, but for maximum impact they would also join the industry-wide effort.

Lobbying for passage of Open Society proposals is a job industry committees might do that's not too different from the lobbying they already do when legislation affecting their interests is before Congress. Let a tariff bill or a trade-regulation bill come to Capitol Hill and Washington is inundated by industry lobbyists. The same kind of unified lobbying activity is needed for legislation affecting the poor and the cities. Prominent businessmen have already spoken out in favor of a negative income tax; organized industry backing for it could get an economic security program through the Congress.

Industry-wide social action committees could also bring about more business investment in the ghetto. It's not a difficult task. Essentially it is the same one companies are doing right now in underdeveloped countries. I know of a case where a Latin-American country made it illegal for foreign-owned companies to import goods on a large scale. One American company decided that, to protect its investment, it had to develop locally owned industry as a source of supplies. It provided loans, technical assistance, training, helped design products and manufacturing equipment, and laid out new plants. It adjusted its own buying schedules to fit the local plant's production schedules, and bought the whole output. Then it reinvested its earnings in the area. Why can't that be done in the ghettos of America? It would create jobs for black workers and also create what is so sorely lacking in the ghetto—a stable managerial and business class.

The ghetto needs large-scale business investment because black businessmen have had such a hard time getting loans and credit. Only one in a thousand black people owns his own business, compared to one out of forty whites. We can equalize those figures if industry will back black-owned-and-operated businesses. One way it can be done quickly is to extend franchising operations to black communities. This is one of the fastest-growing fields today. Instead of setting up branch stores or restaurants in communities, companies sell individuals the right to run one on license, paying a percentage of their income to the parent company. Industry should give black businessmen the opportunity to own these franchises; more, it will have to provide loans so that they can buy the operation; and special job training.

Business can also help the ghetto's economy by buying from black-owned suppliers, and using black architects, contracters, and consultants whenever possible; not just for work within the ghetto—apartheid isn't the answer—but throughout normal operations.

The private sector has two important resources that have to be put to better social use. One is money; the other is managerial skills.

American corporations now donate about $900 million to tax-exempt charities, and educational and health institutions. Most of this giving demonstrates an extraordinary lack of sensitivity to priorities in these troubled times. One Ivy

League college gets more corporate donations to its already-overflowing endowment fund than all the Negro colleges put together. Although business donations to the Urban League have multiplied in the past several years, they represent only a fraction of what we need to expand our job training and community action programs. We're trying to do something about poverty and its roots, but we get less support than do some organizations whose work, however important its backers think it is, have little impact on our society. Too often business giving is subject to the whim of the chief corporate officer. If his mother had a pet dachshund, well, then, the Home for Retired Dachshunds gets a yearly check for $100,000 from his company, while his board worries about riots destroying corporation property. It doesn't make sense. Resources are far too limited for us to be able to afford anything less than maximum effort on all fronts and rational corporate giving is one way for business to have a real impact on society's ills.

Such giving has to be done in a businesslike manner. The woods are full of racial racketeers and self-appointed "leaders" with no followers, and well-meaning businessmen can get their fingers burned. I know of one executive who announced a large gift to a "militant" and then had to face a battery of reporters who wanted to know about the "militant's" charge that strings were attached. The strings turned out to be a simple request, normal with large donations, for an accounting of how funds were spent. When the executive called me for advice, I told him he'd be a fool to give money to someone who wouldn't say what he was using it for; that he had gone out looking for the loudest Negro in town, on the mistaken assumption that this was an indicator of leadership. I left him with the suggestion that while he might get some kicks out of running to the ghetto to talk with leather-jacketed self-styled militants, his donations ought to be organized on a more businesslike basis, with staff delegated to research prospective beneficiaries and accounting procedures established.

Corporate contributions would amount to enough to make a real difference if industry would voluntarily tithe itself. At least 2 per cent of corporate profits could be set aside for socially useful projects, ranging from outright contributions to financing for plants and stores in the ghetto. Two per cent represents a relatively insignificant amount, but it would come to about $2 billion a year. This would be an investment over and above the amount business would ordinarily invest in the ghetto and would not include federally subsidized job or loan programs; it would be an extra dividend that business was contributing toward social stability and progress. Since the bulk of it would be in profit-making investments, corporations would not be asked to make sacrifices; they would only be asked to allocate investments to benefit the whole economy, and not just already-prosperous areas.

Management skills these days go far beyond the simple ledger-keeper of the past. Industry is where we find systems analysts and specialists in administration, production, and public information. Skilled managers are an untapped resource, and business has an obligation to share them with society.

Some companies recognize this and have loaned their brightest and most energetic executives to local governments and voluntary agencies such as the Urban League. Executives on loan to government have reformed local schools and suggested innovations that saved taxpayers millions of dollars, while improving public services.

Business ought to institutionalize these arrangements by offering employees a public-service tour of duty. Capable people who want to take part in social programs should be loaned to government, private agencies, and community councils, with their salaries still paid by the company. Such a program would help industry to attract the bright young idealists who now spurn the business world because they believe it is only interested in piling up profits. During World War II, corporations responded to the crisis by loaning executives to the federal government—the famous dollar-a-year men, so called because their own companies paid their regular salaries while their government pay was a token $1 per year. This, too, is a time of crisis, and business can do as much again. Public and social service is valuable experience in the development of an executive, and I can see how such tours of duty could become choice assignments, eagerly sought after by men on their way to the top.

Education is another area in which companies could make a significant contribution while helping themselves. I've never been able to understand why business, which depends so heavily on the public schools and which pays the bulk of school taxes, has tolerated the ineptitude of what passes for education these days. Most vocational schools, especially, have become day-care centers for teenagers who aren't headed for college. The so-called vocational education they get is usually limited to learning outmoded skills on outmoded machinery. When they graduate, companies have to spend money to train them in the skills that are really needed. Why train twice? Business has to become involved in the schools, contributing machinery and instructors to teach work skills relevant to today's job market.

Some companies, already moving in this direction, have "adopted" schools. They send personnel people to conduct classes in how to get jobs and advise on curriculum; they give the school films and other teaching aids and help graduates find jobs. Other firms are backing nonpublic schools that repair the damage done by the miseducators. The Urban League's street academies, for example, are sponsored by several of the largest corporations in the country; the League's staff runs the schools, and the company picks up the tab. The corporate name on the storefront door of the school it supports tells the community: WE CARE.

Few institutions in our society are so well-equipped to help build an Open Society as labor. Over the years, labor has fought stubbornly for the working man and his right to a share in society's privileges and power. That fight has largely been won; now the union movement has to extend its victories to those of us who are still struggling for the same goals.

One of the most important things labor can do is combat the racism that exists among its members. Just as businessmen are becoming involved in positive ways because of enlightened self-interest, union men should see that their own interests lie in building an Open Society. Labor has done an effective job at times, as witness the 1968 election. In a massive educational campaign that crushed the growing support George Wallace seemed to be getting from blue-collar workers, the AFL–CIO pointed out that Wallace was governor of an antiunion state that kept wages down. Whatever their feelings about race, few workers pulled the Wallace lever in the polling booth. I'd like to see a similar campaign waged in support of the rights of black people. Unionists must come to realize that they too will benefit from the Open Society programs we've suggested, and that the Negro represents not a threat to white workers, but an important ally. Black demands for more jobs, houses, and education benefit all Americans, especially the moderate-income workers who make up the bulk of union membership.

Unions need to be much more aggressive in recruiting black workers for membership and for apprenticeship programs. More Negro union officials are also needed. Unless black people share the positions of power within the labor movement, they will continue to question the sincerity of the liberalism so freely professed by labor leaders.

Perhaps labor's biggest contribution can come from doing what it does best—organizing workers. Just as corporate executives are a major national resource, so also are union organizers. These are men trained to recruit members and to negotiate important matters. A good organizer is one part lawyer, one part social worker, one part manager, and one part father confessor. That's a unique combination, and I'd like to see these talents used to organize tenant unions, neighborhood unions, block cooperatives, unskilled workers, migrant workers, and other groups left out of the prosperous society labor itself has so recently won a place in.

The labor movement can also create an impact through the use of the massive pension funds it has at its disposal. These now amount to billions of dollars and they are invested in everything from corporate stocks to housing developments. A portion of these funds could be invested in ghetto shopping centers, housing, and businesses. Pension funds aren't anything to speculate with, and such investments obviously would have to be chosen carefully, but there is no reason why the ghetto shouldn't get its share of the money now invested in similar enterprises elsewhere.

Churches, too, should use their immense investment portfolios to back slum rehabilitation, integrated housing developments, and other socially beneficial projects. Part of their funds could be placed in black-controlled banks, which provide credit for black businessmen. Churches could use their great wealth as a club to force other institutions to change. As one clergyman told me, "Our investment policy ought to be this—if you don't hire Negroes we won't buy from you; if you don't become involved in social change we won't buy your stock and we will ask our members not to buy your stock or your products; if you won't make loans to blacks, we'll put our money elsewhere." He was aware of the fact that to the businessman, Church Power is Money Power.

It goes without saying that churches should be taking the lead, with integrated memberships and integrated schools that provide subsidies for ghetto children. Churches should be involved in civil rights action programs and in attempts to organize poor communities. But they've also got to go out and fight for social legislation. The Church is a politically powerful institution that can mobilize millions of people to back important bills. Old Guard Congressmen fear this power. Senator Richard Russell was quoted as saying that the Civil Rights Act of 1964 passed because ". . . those damn preachers had got the idea that it was a moral issue."

Race *is* a moral issue. I don't expect other groups to respond to moral appeals, but the Church exists as the caretaker of morality, and it must use its influence to cleanse racism from the minds and souls of its members.

It can only do this if ministers, rabbis, and priests know at a gut-level what it means to be poor and black in a society that is indifferent to poverty and oppressive to black people. All theological students should serve a period of internship in slum churches, even if they don't intend to make their careers in the urban ministry. With this experience and with special training in urban problems and race relations, they can then go on to the churches and synagogues of suburbia to mobilize the support of the affluent behind the urgent needs of the poor.

America's vast communications industry must be the cornerstone of any campaign to educate people for diversity. The media have a special responsibility, because of their unique privileges in our society as the only industry protected by specific constitutional guarantees—the free press clause of the First Amendment. Broadcasters have still another privilege: they use the airwaves—which belong to the public—to conduct their business. Lord Thomson, the Canadian who built a huge communications empire, once said: "A TV license is a license to print money." Special privileges must go hand in hand with special responsibilities to society.

The advertising industry has an awesome power to persuade. Millions of regular television viewers watch six to ten hours of sales pitches a week, and then they go out and buy and, buy and buy. This immense persuasive power could be harnessed to an educational campaign—to show the damage done to every American by racism, the need for action to save our cities—if every major advertiser committed a portion of his advertising budget to the effort. The precedent for this already exists: insurance companies use their ads to teach safe driving. A public service commercial to educate people for diversity would provide the sponsor with all the benefits of institutional advertising. It would tell the public that here is a responsible company (or industry), committed to a better America. If only a small portion of the nearly $18 billion spent on advertising in 1968 were diverted to such a campaign, people's attitudes could be changed.

Educating the public about social issues will take more than a sales campaign. A new approach is needed in the way racial and urban news stories are reported. For too long, news media have hidden behind a façade of "neutrality," pursuing the shibboleth of completely objective reporting. But as one editor said, "In the midst of social cataclysm, telling both sides of the story may not always be telling the truth." The old formulas, which work in covering routine stories, must take a back seat now to new ways of covering the stories that affect our national survival.

I'm not arguing in favor of turning our news media into a propaganda mill. However, I do feel that racial and urban news stories should embody certain assumptions: that a serious economic and social gap exists between the races; that Negroes still do not get equal treatment; that the cities, and consequently the nation, are in a battle for survival; and that resolution of this crisis should be a major national priority. If newsmen made these assumptions their starting point, they would do a much better job of informing and educating an obviously unenlightened public.

This is the way foreign affairs have always been covered. Read any story of a cold-war incident and you find similar assumptions: that the Russians want to dominate the world; that America's security is threatened by communism; and that American military strength and foreign alliances are essential to combat communism. These assumptions aren't limited to the editorial pages; they are implicit in almost any story on foreign affairs. Many people disagree with one or another of these assumptions and experts know they are oversimplified, but they still pervade news reports and nobody objects. I'm asking that this precedent be followed— that we no longer take the misleading "objective" approach to racial and urban stories.

The power of the media to change men's minds is really extraordinary. To continue the foreign-affairs analogy, I can recall when, after the Hitler-Stalin pact, all coverage was anti-Russian. Then, during the war, we were told to love our brave Russian allies. With the start of the cold war, they suddenly became vicious beasts out to destroy us. When international tensions relaxed, we got stories about how liberal Communists were becoming. After tanks moved into Prague, they became villains again. These flip-flops followed whatever line was deemed in the national interest at the time. We are now at a point where the national interest requires a commitment to the humane values of an Open Society and the reeducation of an American public that is, at best, indifferent to racism. Advocacy reporting is standard journalistic practice; it was never more needed than it is now in covering today's racial and urban crisis.

( 2 2 1 )

Specially trained reporters are needed, too. When *The New York Times* assigned one of its top reporters to cover the Supreme Court, it first sent him to law courses. When he was reassigned to a foreign beat, *The Times* hired a lawyer to replace him, because it felt that the Court's rulings could not be adequately reported without an understanding of the legal complexities involved.

Race relations demand the same kind of specialized reporting. The average white reporter, commuting from his suburban home to his desk in the city room, cannot hope to understand the problems of a welfare mother or an unemployed man in the ghetto. The special circumstances of the Negro community can be understood only by people with training and sensitivity. They are not to be found in our newsrooms today in the numbers they are needed.

Race relations should be a special news beat, just as City Hall and other sectors are the province of specialists. Reporters on that beat need to be selected for their sensitivity, and should be given special training—courses in race relations, urban problems, and Negro history, among others. They could be assigned to work for a while with civil rights and community action agencies to gain contacts, experience, and an understanding of the Negro's point of view.

A top newspaper would not think of sending a correspondent to Moscow without special training in the language and history of Russia, and the chosen reporter would invariably be one of experience and reliability. Yet the same newspaper often thinks nothing of sending a cub reporter to cover a story of social change in the ghetto. Since Americans have made a foreign country out of the ghetto, our newspapers need to give reporters in Harlem and Hough the same preparation they give to their reporters in Moscow and Paris.

## RESPONSIBILITY FOR CHANGE

The communications industry must insure that journalism schools offer courses in racial and urban problems: more, urban affairs institutes are needed to offer specialized training for reporters and to provide syndicated facts and stories about urban affairs that smaller papers and broadcasters could use.

Special efforts—recruitment, training, assistance to predominately Negro liberal arts schools—should be made to attract black reporters and production and administrative staff. The media are in somewhat the same position baseball was in in 1947, when the Brooklyn Dodgers made Jackie Robinson the first black major-leaguer. Because other teams were slow to hire other black players, the Dodgers soon cornered the market and were able to dominate the game for years. There's a chance now for some company to become the Brooklyn Dodgers—*circa* 1947—of the communications field.

The broadcasting industry has a special responsibility to stop air pollution—the hate-filled slanders that pour out over the airwaves. Some stations run prepackaged programs supplied by syndicated extremists, while others, in their unending pursuit of the unusual and the sensational, open their microphones to a variety of bigots and racists, especially in the popular "talk" shows. Some stations are openly biased. The United Church of Christ brought documented complaints against a Mississippi television station that consistently programmed anti-Negro materials. Its license was still renewed. A license isn't a right, it's a privilege, and when it is abused in this manner it ought to be taken away from the offender. Broadcasters who discriminate in hiring should also lose their licenses. Aggressive action by the FCC is needed here, and one way to get it may be to appoint, at long last, at least one black man to the FCC. Black people depend on radio more than any other medium, yet the regulatory agency supposed to protect the rights of listeners has never had a black Commissioner.

The FCC could be more than a policing body. It could help mobilize the broadcasting industry to provide technical assistance and training for community-operated television stations. Few UHF channels are now in use, nor are they economically feasible for commercial broadcasters at this time. Empty channels represent a waste of natural resources. They could be used by the community as a forum of ideas for educational programs such as courses in reading and math, as an information service listing available jobs and apartments, and for the nonprofessional creative talents of the community. Television ought to become a force for involving people with each other and with their community.

## WHAT YOU, AS AN INDIVIDUAL, CAN DO

We've made lots of proposals for changing the racist behavior of the institutions that control our lives, but it is vital that the actions and attitudes of individual Americans change too. They must, if we are to become an Open Society free from the fear, the insecurity, and the brutality that racism breeds.

The vast silent mass of Americans—those who have never committed themselves either to overt racism or to active involvement in the cause of civil rights—will now have to stand up and be counted. They must prove that the hearts and minds of men *can* be changed, and that the majority of

# RESPONSIBILITY FOR CHANGE

Americans aren't content to be moral vegetables, indifferent to the injustice around them or to the potentialities for a better society.

Some people believe that attitudes can't be changed. I disagree; I've seen people do an about-face overnight when their own self-interest was at stake. When the Brooklyn Dodgers brought the first Negro, Jackie Robinson, into the major leagues, they had plenty of southern ballplayers who swore they'd never play with a black man. But as soon as Robinson started hitting those home runs and stealing bases, their attitudes changed. They realized that they could stick with Robinson and share some World Series money through his efforts, or they could go back to Mississippi to push a plow. That was one change of attitude that didn't take long.

When I was in Vietnam I met a white soldier from Mississippi who had just arrived at the front. He had no combat experience and was scared out of his wits, but his black sergeant, a hardened veteran of guerrilla warfare, knew the jungle like the back of his hand. That young fellow stuck to the sergeant like glue. He couldn't do enough for him, *sir*ing him left and right. He had made a simple choice—he knew he could be a dead bigoted white boy from Mississippi, or a live liberal white boy from Mississippi. The prejudices of twenty years melted away when survival was at stake.

Our society has that choice. It can die clinging to its bigotry or it can breathe freely in an atmosphere free of racism. The choice really is one of survival, and each and every one of us has a responsibility to ourselves and to our children to keep this society alive by transforming it.

Most people will agree that institutions should be changed and laws passed, but when it comes to individual action, paralysis sets in. "Who, me?" they ask. "I'm just one person, what can I do?" The answer is "Plenty."

The place to start is in the home. Racism is one disease most people don't make special efforts to prevent. Their children are inoculated against polio and smallpox, but somehow they are expected to avoid catching the racism that pervades the whole society without any special preventive measures being taken. People think that because they never use the word *nigger* at home, their children won't be prejudiced. That's like saying we don't invite typhoid carriers into our home. Of course not; but we do inoculate our children against typhoid so they won't catch it when they do run into a Typhoid Mary. Racism is a disease—a major public health problem—and parents must vaccinate their children against it with strong, positive attitudes toward race so that when they get out into society they can throw off racism as if it were any of the viruses they've been inoculated against.

The way to build these attitudes is by example, and the way to start is by demonstrating your own respect for all people, whatever their race or position in life. Most Americans aren't even aware of the subtle racism so casually accepted by whites and blacks alike, and expressed over and over in small things, such as calling a maid by her first name.

Some time ago, my wife and I employed a lady to do housework for us one day a week. The first day she came, she introduced herself as "Mary."

My wife asked: "What is your last name?"

"Smith," she said, and looked rather surprised.

When my two children came home from school, my wife introduced them.

"Lauren and Marcia, this is Mrs. Smith."

"You don't have to do that, Mrs. Young," she said. "I like to be called Mary. It makes me feel more comfortable, like one of the family, and I can relate better to the children. And, after all, all white people call me Mary."

My wife said: "We are not doing this for you, as much as we respect you; we're doing it for our children. We don't permit them to call a forty- or forty-five-year-old woman by her first name. We don't let them call any of our friends by their first names. We're trying to teach them that there is no difference between people because of the color of their skin or the kind of work they do."

An hour later, Mrs. Smith's ten-year-old son telephoned the house and asked for Mary.

"I'm sorry, but there's no Mary here," my wife said, and hung up. Then she told Mrs. Smith she thought the call had been from her son and suggested that she call him back.

"Mama," the boy said, "they told me there was no Mary there."

"And there isn't," his mother told him, with pride in her voice. "In this house I am somebody. Here I am Mrs. Smith."

First-naming black domestic servants is a custom. We permit it to go on without thinking about it. We have caught the disease because this is a diseased society. And first-naming is only part of the problem. It is also customary to pay low wages to black domestic workers, to provide no paid vacations or holidays—and conveniently to "forget" to pay the employer's social security tax, though this is required by law.

Children also need to see black people in roles other than those of servant or janitor. They will see through their parents' hypocrisy if, in spite of a lot of high-sounding talk about equality, black people are never guests in the home. It is important for children to have tangible evidence that blacks are their peers. Someone who has never had black friends may find that it's not easy to begin. Sometimes extra effort is needed to overcome uncomfortable mutual suspicions. The black man may guess that such an invitation is unusual, and he may resent being somebody's Exhibit A for the evening. But the effort by both sides is worth it, because blacks, no less than whites, need to establish interracial contacts and get past the hollow formality that so often marks social life between the races. The white person may spend the day worrying about what he should talk about. "Shall I tell him how sorry I was about Dr. King?" But 99 per cent of the time, the talk, once started, will settle comfortably into mutual-interest areas—bowling scores or gripes about what a louse the boss is.

The big difficulty in such social relations is the very fact that they *are* unusual, that people feel they have to act differently or otherwise be on their best behavior, unable to relax. I recall a fellow who sat next to me on a flight who asked if he might discuss a problem of his with me. Since I've found that seatmates in airplanes won't hear your "No," I said that I was all ears.

"It's about my wife," he said. "We're both great liberals, and we'd like very much to invite a Negro couple to our home sometime, but my wife doesn't feel comfortable around Negroes—I hope you're not offended. What can I do about this?"

"I'm not offended," I told him as I watched him wade into his second martini. "Most people feel inferior around a man like Ralph Bunche—a brilliant man who has been friends with diplomats, presidents, and kings. I can see why she'd feel inferior around him. Why doesn't she come to the Urban League, and we'll help her identify some below-average Negroes with whom she'd feel more comfortable."

The point is very simple. There is no such thing as *a* Negro, any more than there is a white person or a Republican. People come in all sizes and shapes, bright and dumb, liberal and conservative. I don't think that anyone who is sincere about living—as well as talking—democratically, would have any trouble making friends with people of like interests of other races.

Still another way for families to become involved is to write their congressmen. I know it sounds corny, but you'd be surprised at the influence Congressional mail can have. It helped to pass the civil rights bills and it can help to pass economic security programs, home-building plans, and other important attempts to close the gap between white and black, rich and poor. Some congressmen are scared rabbits. They know they're up for election every two years and they're anxious not to alienate their constituents. If they are convinced there is support for a measure (and the only way for them to tell is to count their mail), they'll support it even if they don't feel strongly about it themselves.

Reactionaries are always writing letters—the right wing must have lots of people with nothing else to do. But these kook letters and form letters are standard stuff and congressmen don't take them seriously any more. What they do take seriously is the obviously earnest letter from a long-silent voter asking them to support a social-reform measure. Especially if they are from fairly conservative districts, such letters will have impact if there are enough of them. Congress beat back open housing legislation in 1967. Later it was flooded with mail from thousands of individuals who asked passage of an open housing bill as a memorial to Dr. King, and it passed a far stronger bill than had been beaten down a few months before. Don't underestimate the power of the pen: politicians make their living by responding to the popular will.

There's a lot people can do, from letter-writing campaigns to all the single, seemingly insignificant acts that, when taken together, add up to basic changes in the ways whites and blacks live together.

Here are a number of these things that you, the reader, can do. The possibilities are limitless, so this is not a comprehensive list, but it will do for a start.

• *Communicate. Listen* to what black people are saying. Really listen—to the emotions behind the words, to the desire to communicate that often hides behind words of anger, to the need to be equal that hides behind talk of disgust with White America. Listen and understand. Educate yourself and pass your insights on to others.

• *Learn* about the contributions black people have made. It will help you to place the present crisis in context. Check out your children's textbooks—make sure that they are learning about black contributions to America and not about Sambo's happy slavehood.

• *Help black people get jobs.* You don't have to be an employer yourself. Next time you are at the supermarket ask the manager why there are no black workers there, if that's the case. Write your utility company to ask why you've never seen a black meter-reader or repairman. Become color-conscious in the establishments you frequent—it's no accident if your favorite restaurant doesn't have black waiters or your favorite store has no black salespeople. Ask questions about it and write some letters. It's possible the managers never thought about it and will be moved to hire blacks now that you've called it to their attention. More likely, they were fearful of customer reaction, and your queries will reassure them. This can have an effect far beyond just jobs. When people see an all-white staff in a store they assume that's right and proper. People go along with what is, and you can help to change things so that what is is what should be.

• *Boycott.* Letter-writing is great for rainy days, and businesses, especially, fear customer complaints. If you read that a company has been cited for discrimination, let them know you won't buy their goods any more: boycott. On the other hand, when a company is outstanding in this field, let them know you appreciate their efforts—and let their competitors know that's your reason for buying from the more responsible company.

• *Buy black.* Black businessmen often have markets limited to impoverished ghetto areas. They need to serve the whole society, not just a segment of it. Black contractors, painters, servicemen, etc., are as good as any others. Discriminate.

• *Volunteer.* Most people have skills that can be put to good use. The Urban League's nearly 100 affiliates and national office have about 8000 people who are volunteer workers, some of them full-time. You can tutor ghetto kids, teach your trade at a community center, type in a community office. It's a rare person who has nothing he can teach someone else, no service he can perform for groups short of staff. Men can supervise recreational activities, women can teach homemaking skills. The list is endless—and someone, somewhere, could use your knowledge and experience. Remember that good volunteers simply offer their skills, they don't try to tell people what to do. No missionaries need apply.

• *Invest in integrated institutions.* Your savings would earn the same interest in a black-owned bank that does make loans to ghetto businesses as they earn now in a downtown bank that doesn't. The same federal insurance applies, too, so you risk nothing while your money helps revive the ghetto's economy. If you buy stocks, investigate some of the companies that specialize in integrated housing investments and similar enterprises.

• *Educate other white people.* Don't close your ears when you hear bigoted remarks. Racism becomes more respectable when it goes unchallenged. Most people are simply ignorant of the facts. When they complain "We made it, why can't they?" tell them why and break the racial code language. Phrases like *law and order* are used in distorted ways. "Crime in the streets" often means "Keep blacks from protesting injustices." "Neighborhood schools" often means "Keep black kids out of our schools."

Eddies of racial bigotry swirl around most people every day. The material in the Introduction and first two chapters of this book gave you ammunition for many a good argument. The important thing to remember is that these falsehoods flourish because people think they can get away with them. When you are silent, they assume you agree, and thus you lend encouragement to bigots.

• *Bring open housing to your neighborhood.* Most white people live in ghettos of their own, gilded though they may be. You and your neighbors can put pressure on your landlord or on local realtors not to discriminate. Pass information of housing vacancies on to the Urban League's Operation Equality or to your local fair housing committee. Volunteer to work with such groups; you'll find it interesting. You can be a "checker"—someone who verifies that an apartment is available so that when the fair housing people send black house-hunters to apply and they're turned down, discrimination can be proved. Or you can do some of the office work that's so necessary. If your community has no such group, organize one yourself. Most of the work is education—convincing people to rent and sell to black people.

• *Desegregate your job, your school, your club, your professional organization.* Suggest to your employer that he start training programs or recruit workers through the Urban League or other community groups. Be active in your union or club to try to get black members. Tell your minister that it's a sin that the church's congregation is all white and that it doesn't engage in social action. Sponsor black members and invite black guests to your country club. Some suburbanites with big back yards and swimming pools invite ghetto kids to use them. One woman who thought she was being daring by doing this was a bit worried about what her neighbors would say. It turned out they were so impressed that the whole neighborhood was opened up and back yards were filled with the laughter of ghetto children frolicking in pools with their delighted hosts.

• *Use your power.* Many people excel in one area or another, and they have a degree of power. They may be especially respected by their neighbors, have responsible jobs, work in government, own shares in companies, or they're active in their churches. Use this prestige, influence, or power to open up jobs for blacks or to get your organization involved in social action. The man who owns ten shares of stock in a major corporation may not think he has power, but if he asks the company president at a stockholder's meeting why the firm has such a bad hiring record and is not involved in social programs, the president will be put on the spot in public—and the press will be there, too. You can help your club or union organize adult education programs dealing with race relations and the urban crisis, with ghetto leaders invited to lecture and answer questions. Help your church, club, or union develop some of the programs that are open to nonprofit organizations, such as federally subsidized nonprofit housing.

These are just a few of the things concerned individuals can do. There are others. Every locality has different conditions and different problems, but concerned citizens can always find ways to help. Shortly after Dr. King's death I received a letter—one of literally thousands—asking how the writer could help. "I live in an area where there aren't any Negroes, but I want to do *something*," she said. I was going to advise her to invest in integrated firms and to write to businesses and her local authorities when it occurred to me to check on who her congressman was. As I expected, it was an individual who is usually described as a "moderate conservative," just the kind of person whose outlook is decent and reasonable. Since there are so very few Negroes in his rural northern district, he had never become involved in social legislation that would help the cities. He had voted for some bills and against others. If he could be won over to support open housing or economic security programs, it would be more than just another Congressional vote. He was respected and had good committee assignments. A change of heart on his part and he might sway other fence-sitting congressmen like him. My letter-writer thought that "doing something" meant that there had to be a ghetto nearby, when the most valuable thing she could do would be to organize people who thought the way she did and put some pressure on her congressman.

"Where there's a will, there's a way," goes the old saying. If you have the will to become involved and just don't know where to begin, here are a few more pointers:

• You can volunteer your skills through established organizations, which will either accept your services or refer you to another organization that will. Your church, school, and local community action organization are good places to start. Nearby health and welfare agencies are listed in the phone book, or the local government office that deals with health and welfare can give you some tips.

• Volunteer directly to ghetto institutions. Ghetto churches and schools can either use your help or refer you to someone who can. Obvious places to go are your local Urban League, NAACP, or community action agency.

• The mayor's office or governor's office can refer you to agencies in your community that can use your help. So can federal agencies such as the Office of Economic Opportunity.

• If you are a businessman, you can volunteer management assistance to ghetto businesses through the Interracial Council on Business Opportunities or similar programs.

In the final analysis, anyone who does not respond to the

terrible poverty and discrimination that are everywhere in this land of affluence is in worse shape than the victims. Nobody knows this better than your children—they believe in civil rights and human dignity. They want to be shown that you care, that you are involved. Many people aren't happy about some of the things their kids are doing, but, with Anatole France, I prefer the errors of enthusiasm to the indifference of wisdom, for a society that permits an excess of indifference needs more than anything else an excess of caring. An ancient Greek scholar once was asked when justice would come to Athens. He replied, "When those who are not injured are as indignant as those who are." So shall it be here in America.

## BLACK POWER AND SOCIAL CHANGE

Black Americans have a special responsibility: to fight for their own freedom. Freedom is never simply given, it must be won. Unless a unified, organized black community insists, the individuals and institutions who hold power in our society will not change. The next few crucial years will demand of black Americans an iron determination to win equality, coupled with the flexibility to form coalitions with the white community around issues of importance to the ghetto. Such a strategy demands discipline and responsible action.

It is much easier to stand on a street corner and curse "whitey" or to call for violent rebellion than it is to engage in the hard work of building real power by organizing the skills of the community and by negotiating with potential allies among the white majority. But the enemies of black freedom aren't afraid of lung power or even the feeble fire power some extremists boast of. These only become justifications for further suppression and for use of indiscriminate violence against black people. We saw that White America didn't hesitate to use its superior arsenal during the riots of the past several years. Some people thought White Power could be overthrown by threats and Molotov cocktails, but the tanks and armed troops that occupied riot-battered ghettos were evidence enough that violence can't work.

What the enemies of black freedom do fear are brain power, economic power, and political power. These will grow as black Americans continue to develop their own sense of pride, and most of all, a new sense of community. Black people can no longer afford to fight each other or fall into the pit of generalizing about all white people that prevents the establishment of important ties with decent white Americans who help us to overcome the evils in our society.

The history of the term *Black Power* offers insights into the dangers of navigating the rocky shoals of racism. Black Power has meant all things to all people. To the black militants who created the term, it meant separation from an evil white society bent on suppressing black people, and it meant the expulsion of whites from the civil rights movement. To white liberals, it meant fear and black abandonment of integration. To white racists, it meant that at last black people would no longer ask to share real power in this society. They were only too glad to have blacks turn back in on themselves, acquiescing in American apartheid by a retreat into the ghetto.

My own feeling at the time was one of misgiving. I saw that it was possible that the hopes of white racists would be fulfilled, and that Black Power would indeed mean a retreat from meaningful change, trading the real power that comes from full equality in a pluralistic society for the shadow power of self-segregated black reservations. And as the term came to be associated with self-destructive violence and with angry threats, the prospect of losing important support within the white community became more real.

Black Power, of course, was what we had always been fighting for. Nobody was for integration because sitting next to white people in schools or at lunch counters was a great experience. Integration was a means to full participation in all areas of life, and to a share of the power in America. Other groups had the same ends, but they didn't shout Irish Power or Jewish Power. They "integrated" or infiltrated the institutions of society until they had power. Power is something you use, not talk about.

As the term took root, however, it became essential to re-examine its meaning. It became necessary to rescue the term from the aura of violence and hostility it was coming to represent. For Black Power is a valuable concept, with roots among black thinkers going back to Frederick Douglass. It is a concept that is relevant to our times and our struggle.

Black Power can be—and should be—interpreted to mean the development of black pride and self-determination. It means that black people must control their own destiny and their communities. It means the mobilization of black political and economic strength to win complete equality.

This interpretation of Black Power and the relevance of the term rest on two stubborn facts: The ghetto is here to stay for some time to come—for as long as it takes to build an

Open Society and change the behavior of institutions and the minds of men; and, second, it is not possible for a weakened, deprived minority bearing the scars of oppression to "integrate" immediately with a confident, affluent majority society on equal terms.

The ultimate goal for black Americans, as for white Americans, must be the creation of an Open Society. Black Power offers a means to this end, for the primary task today is to build the institutions and the strengths that will enable black Americans to enter an Open Society as equals.

For black Americans the fight for equality must be a war fought on several fronts. The strategy's first front calls for creative confrontations with White America; we must infiltrate its institutions and create the pressures and alliances that will force it to change, taking advantage of every opportunity that opens up, and using every legal means.

Exercising freedoms is like exercising muscles—they atrophy when they are not used. Black Americans can no longer afford to take refuge in safe, traditional jobs that offer no more than security. It is pointless to complain about discrimination in high-paying craft jobs and then not apply for them when, after great legal and persuasive efforts, they become open to black workers. Bright youngsters have to see beyond teaching or the ministry when the money and the power in our society are in finance and big business. The battle for black power has to be fought within the power centers of White America. This means that black people must participate fully in every aspect of American life. It means pioneering—applying for jobs and clubs and homes and schools that have been closed to blacks in the past. To refuse to do this is to acquiesce in White America's belief that blacks are inferior, unable to compete in an Open Society.

As new opportunities open up, they must be seen as beachheads for further forays into the corridors of white power. Some will condemn these opportunities because they are so modest or so isolated in the general pattern of discrimination, but there are always those among us who prefer arguments about abstractions to the hard work of actually changing society.

We must pursue black excellence—the special responsibility to excel: to outthink, outperform, and outdo those who would deny to black people freedom.

When opportunities aren't available, the black community must apply pressures to create them. Peaceful demonstrations are still a weapon, but there are also other ways to move institutions. Boycotts, for example. The boycott is an effective, legal weapon. Not too long ago, the steel companies boosted prices and the administration proudly used the boycott as a weapon to force them to back down, canceling orders from the price-raising companies. There is no reason in the world why black people should not organize to boycott companies that don't hire black workers. This is a way to use real power—economic power—to force change. In Dr. King's Operation Breadbasket in Chicago, the black community refused to do business with firms that discriminated. This approach requires a disciplined black community as well as skilled negotiators who can get the facts about hiring practices and organize the power of the community to force change.

The war for equality must also be waged on another front: in the ghetto itself. We must mobilize the black community to assume control of the ghetto's institutions and to develop the inner strength and unity without which change will remain forever out of reach. At the present time, the ghetto suffers from fragmentation. Leadership is diffuse, energies are squandered or consumed by the day-to-day struggle for survival, and the real power is wielded by institutions that are not responsive to the needs of the black community. An awakened black community participating fully in the control of its own economic, educational, and political resources could transform ghetto life.

This does not imply a retreat into separatism, nor does it imply acceptance of the present system of apartheid. It is a recognition of the facts of life in America today. So long as black people are segregated into racial ghettos, without control over their own lives, the poverty and hopelessness that characterize life in ghetto slums will increase. It is absolutely essential that black Americans assume control of ghetto institutions while at the same time making every effort to enter the mainstream of American life. It's got to be a double-pronged effort. Integration is no longer the issue; the issue today is equality—equal results—and any and all strategies that will bring it about must be used. It may be that a period of self-development and ghetto rehabilitation will coincide with a temporary decline in efforts at integration, but such a period should be seen not as a retreat, but as a strength-gathering preliminary to building a pluralistic society.

Both efforts—moving into the mainstream and turning inward to rebuild the ghetto—must be informed with a sense of black consciousness and group identity. Black men must recognize their obligation to work toward the betterment of the entire black community. Blacks have suffered from the lack of such awareness in the past. Black politicians either sought personal power or submitted to the bidding of white-controlled political machines, and the black community, which voted them into positions of power, got none of the rewards. Chicago's South Side provides dependable majorities for Mayor Richard Daley's powerful machine, but despite the vote-getting efforts of black precinct captains, councilmen, and others, Chicago's black people get little of the patronage such political regularity bestows on other groups.

Black professional people—businessmen, unionists, and others—have to work to change the system and open it up for other black people. The development of "black caucuses" within unions, professional associations, and other groups shows that there is a new awareness that what might be in the narrower interests of the group may not be in the interests of black people. New York's black policemen, for example, broke with the policemen's association and supported the civilian review board. Black teachers refused to back their union's strike against community control of the schools in New York. Black social workers in Chicago refused to make the midnight "man-in-the-house" raids that so degraded their clients.

These are healthy developments, for they signify the end of an era. They are examples of the constructive use of Black Power to influence America's institutions.

Commitment to black solidarity is not reverse racism or mere chauvinism. It's a survival technique, a weapon in the arsenal blacks must use for self-protection and group advancement. In the fight for survival in which the black community is now engaged, every rational weapon must be used and the strongest of these are group consciousness, group solidarity, and group pride.

The middle class bears a special responsibility: to become involved in the problems of the ghetto. There are signs that what used to be called the "black bourgeoisie" is now actually more militant than many other elements in the community. A survey by a Harvard professor, Gary T. Marx, found twice as many "militants" among black professionals as it did among service workers. Comparisons of college graduates and black people whose education stopped at the sixth grade found three times as many "militants" among the college graduates. It is the man who dares to hope, the man who meets the outward requirements for success in our society, who has the least patience.

He is just as angry as the man who is jobless. That anger builds as he sees white people with fewer qualifications than he has get the promotions he deserves. He won't be mollified if the boss takes him out for a drink and stammers excuses about how the stockholders aren't ready for a Negro vice-president or about how contributions to the college building fund will fall off if he's made dean. And he's too smart to waste his anger throwing bricks. He will fight the racist establishment on its own terms, and he can provide much of the leadership the black community needs.

Too many people in the black middle class have been preoccupied with guilt feelings because of charges that they've been aping white values and that they haven't been relevant to the needs of the ghetto. Too many let themselves be intimidated by those who say "The only way you can help me is to get rid of your wealth and be like me."

A good friend of mine who is one of the few black executives of a top corporation was at a meeting during which a ghetto "militant" started condemning the black middle class in just those terms.

"I may be middle-class," my friend responded, "but I haven't always been middle-class. I ate neckbones and rice and there were six kids in my family, and I worked and scraped all through school, delivering papers and shining shoes. I helped my mother feed our family. I went on to Fisk and fought my way into the middle class; so don't tell me I can't identify. I can. But if you think for one moment that, in order to get you to relate to me, I'm going back to those neckbones, you're crazy. I'm going to keep on eating steaks, and I'll help you to get to where you can too, but no more neckbones for me."

His antagonist was utterly destroyed. "You're all right," he said, and then they all got back to the real purpose of the meeting, which was to unify the community.

The black man who has made it into the middle class has a responsibility to assert himself and to reach out a helping hand to his black brother in the ghetto. He has to take his own skills and knowledge about how the system works, the know-how that has helped him to succeed, and help others get it. He can play a role in voluntary organizations and do all the things we've asked white individuals to do, and more. For his own satisfaction, his own conscience, and to earn the respect of his children, he's got to pull his share in making the black community self-reliant and strong.

At the same time, he has a responsibility to excel in his profession. It's not enough to say "I've gone pretty far—for a Negro." That's what many whites are saying about him. He's got to use his skills to show that black people can compete and come out on top. It's gratifying to see, in the past several years, that black social workers, educators, and public health doctors have been elected by their peers—predominantly white—to positions of leadership in their professions. This kind of success places the black man in a position where he can work from the inside to change a predominately white institution, to make it—whether it's a corporation or a professional association—relevant to civil rights.

I can't stress too strongly the need for black people to get top corporate and government jobs. This is the only way to get real economic power. I'm not underestimating the importance of having more black-owned businesses and black-managed plants in the ghetto. Both will open up new opportunities for some people and bring a measure of stability and pride to the ghetto. They are very important, but they don't create that many new jobs.

Most people, for example, when they talk of ghetto-owned businesses, are really talking about the corner grocery or the neighborhood cleaner. Such businesses are marginal at best; the owners have to work long hours and the most they can hope for is a modest income, about what a high-paying factory job brings for fewer hours and less headaches. Black ownership of such establishments creates few jobs. Even small ghetto industrial plants would provide less than fifty or a hundred new jobs per plant. They are important, even necessary, but no one should be fooled into thinking that such modest ventures represent "black capitalism." Real economic power in our society is wielded by giant corporations, which employ many thousands of people. Their employees have the high salaries and fringe benefits that rich companies and union contracts bestow. The vice-president in charge of personnel of one of these companies (or the hiring officer of a government agency) can create more new jobs for black people with the stroke of a pen than can be created through years of painstaking efforts to establish small ghetto businesses.

Any healthy economy—and that includes the potentially healthy ghetto economy—needs both types of economic development: locally owned and operated businesses, and full participation in the larger economy. It would be a mistake for us to get so hung up on romantic ideas of "black capitalism" that we put all our energies into taking over marginal city businesses, left behind by whites who have fled to the suburbs. Today, economic power is vested in managers, not in entrepreneurs.

It's also worth remembering that making a business black-owned or black-operated won't necessarily make it better. Black people have always patronized black businesses. In the South, the only restaurants, theatres, stores, schools we could go to were black-operated and while some were better, others were often worse. And black ownership doesn't necessarily mean the end of exploitation. When the Industrial Union Department of the AFL–CIO set to work in Chicago to organize tenants' unions, black slum landlords talked their tenants into refusing to sign up. They used the argument: "What do you want to get mixed up with white folks for? We can settle this ourselves." This successful appeal to racial solidarity enabled them to go on exploiting other black people.

This is one reason why I am so strongly in favor of elected community councils that would sponsor cooperative ventures. We'd be getting away from possibly exploitive individual ownership and operation, and would create institutions owned and operated by—and responsible to—the entire community. But it must be an organized community, unified behind responsible leadership.

The whole question of leadership is vital at a time when nearly anyone loud enough or bold enough can proclaim himself a "leader." We can't sit back and allow unrepresentative elements to speak for the whole community. We've seen white people intimidated by the threats and demogoguery of small but vocal minorities such as the Klan and the White Citizens' Councils. We can't afford to let that happen to us. The field is full of hustlers and charlatans who don't really care about the black community, but who want power and publicity. I recall one recent incident: A Planned Parenthood group announced plans to provide birth-control information for ghetto mothers. Within hours a virtual unknown called a press conference to denounce the proposal as "genocide" and a white attempt to kill off future black generations. It took determined action by ghetto mothers to convince the public that this man didn't speak for them or for anyone other than himself, and that they had the same rights to family-planning service that middle-class white women have. Black people must speak out, as these women did, when other blacks attempt to exploit them.

The responsibility doesn't stop at denouncing false leaders. On the positive side, black people must actively back community leadership and support the national civil rights organizations, helping them to become more effective and to represent the real interests of the community.

The national organizations are going through a difficult

period now, reexamining their traditional functions and policies and devising new strategies to meet the changing times. We've had our Selmas, our Birminghams, even our Marches on Washington. We have awakened the conscience of the nation and legal barriers to equal rights have largely melted away. But these victories exposed other problems that can't be solved by opening up lunch counters to blacks. The need now is not to challenge the morality of an America that openly segregates blacks by law, but to force the white holders of power to share it, and to transform the life of the ghetto.

A few years ago an organization that marched and demonstrated was called militant, and one that didn't was labeled moderate. Today, I don't know of a single "moderate" organization or leader. We are all angry. We are all determined to lead a responsibly militant black community in a fight for power and justice.

I sense a general realization these days that the various civil rights groups agree more often than they differ, and I see a greater willingness to accept the differences that do exist, recognizing that we don't have to have complete agreement. The black community is in the midst of a war against racism. As in any other war, there has to be a division of responsibilities and there has to be mutual support. The Navy doesn't conduct paratroop operations and the Air Force doesn't fight sea battles; each does what it's trained and equipped to do, and each service on occasion backs up the other. The infantry will call in air strikes to support ground troops and the Navy will shell antiaircraft batteries from offshore to support the Air Force. The civil rights organizations must function as efficiently, each with its own special area of competence, each lending support when needed to the other groups.

Each of the major organizations is uniquely equipped to deal with certain problems facing black citizens. The NAACP, for example, is responsible, through its lawsuits, for many of the advances of the past half-century. The legal battle for civil rights has now largely been won, and I think that the NAACP, in choosing new goals and a new direction, may well decide that its future lies in conducting the political thrust of black Americans. Among all the national organizations, it is uniquely qualified to do this, with some 1800 branches across the country, mostly volunteer-led. This represents an extraordinary pool of volunteer help—to get out the vote, register people, and to apply political pressure.

Black Power is sometimes indistinguishable from Ballot Power, and registering and voting black people is one of the most important tasks facing us. The roughly 8 million black voters are concentrated in large cities in key states and could hold the balance of power in many state and city elections. Black voters in the South have elected black sheriffs and state officials and have even forced white politicians to mind their pronunciation of *Negro*. Even George Wallace painstakingly pronounces it "Knee-grow" so that the traditional "nigra" won't offend black voters. But the value of the black vote is not in its effect on a politician's elocution but on his desire to be re-elected. We need to register more black voters, get them to the polls, and identify for them those representatives who have done a good job for us and those who haven't, so that our friends can be rewarded and our enemies punished. Monitoring enforcement of civil rights laws and testing their effectiveness is another need. At the same time, there has to be extensive lobbying in Washington and in state capitols—lobbying so well organized that immediate pressure can be brought to bear on key congressmen whenever necessary.

In the Southern Christian Leadership Conference, Dr. Martin Luther King, Jr., left behind a unique structure for change. Made up primarily of ministers, it will continue to challenge the conscience of the country and particularly its religious institutions. But I think that the SCLC, probing in its turn for new directions, may come more and more often to use its moral force and its special ability to reach people to organize specific local actions such as boycotts. In the past we've had small, loosely organized groups announce boycotts against an industry or company. Often they couldn't bring it off; it was bad strategy, anyway. A corporation that may be guilty of discrimination in one city might be the best example of fair employment in another. The boycott is more effective when it zeros in on a particular business, documents the degree of discrimination practiced, points out how much of the company's income comes from black people, and then rouses the support of the community to make the company change. The churches, with their regular membership, their discipline, and their custom of presenting reports, can use this kind of tactic beautifully. SCLC's many young activist ministers can also play a major role in organizing the black community and in articulating its needs and desires.

It is vitally important to continue to involve young people in programs of social change. This is what the Student Non-Violent Co-ordinating Committee did so well in the early 'sixties with its sit-ins and summer projects for both white and black youths. We now realize that, while bringing busloads of white students to Mississippi is no longer the answer, it is vital to involve black students in community organization and white students in educating other whites to the dangers of racism. SNCC is going through a transitional period these days, but ultimately I would expect that present youth groups will be taken over by the young leaders coming out of our colleges who are now active in the black student associations on campus.

SNCC lost much of its following because it was unable to find a role for itself that would make its Black Power sloganeering relevant to today's realities. CORE, which also adopted the Black Power slogan at the outset, is today concerned with translating it into effective programming. It is important that real black power—in the form of expanded ghetto entrepreneurship, consumer-co-operatives, and economic development—be given the full-time attention of at least one organization that would aim at developing black involvement. CORE, through projects in selected cities, is already moving in that direction.

The Urban League has also gone through a period of self-examination and self-renewal. In at least one respect, it differs from other civil rights organizations: it is a professional agency staffed by experts in economic-development, education, health, and welfare programs. Like other agencies, we have volunteer help, but our staff of 800 is all skilled professionals.

The Urban League is also the agency that has the strongest contacts with the Establishment. Because of its long-standing dedication to interracial teamwork, it is in the best position to challenge white leadership when challenge is needed, and to assist when assistance is in order.

The Urban League's major new goal is to develop an organizational base in the black community. Our professional staff can help the ghetto select or develop its own authentic leadership. We can provide the community with expert help in documenting its demands, and then arrange for its leaders to confront the white holders of power. Our experience can insure that these confrontations become negotiating sessions, not just shouting matches. We do not propose to speak for black people—no one individual or organization has the right to do that—but to work with black people and local black leadership.

The Urban League must also continue to challenge America's institutions with experimental programs that both demonstrate the need for new techniques and offer remedies for institutional failures. Our street-academy program is one example of this. Educating hundreds of high school dropouts is important, but its real value lies in challenging the system. However, the success of the street academies also demonstrates that these youngsters *can* succeed academically—to the point of graduating from Harvard. We have not only demolished the myth that black kids are slow learners and not interested in school, but we have also shown the public schools how to change their practices. Our job-training programs do the same thing for industry: they demonstrate that given half a chance black people are eager, dependable, skilled workers, and they challenge businesses to set up similar programs.

The need for co-operation among the various national civil rights groups and among community groups is obvious. The Urban League's professional expertise in community organization and its links to white institutions can be invaluable aids to groups that specialize in ghetto self-development projects. Our job-training and job-locating programs, now highly effective in the 100 cities in which we operate, could be extended to the NAACP's massive base in 1800 communities. Such co-ordinated efforts are absolutely necessary today. The particular skills and historic concerns of each of the national organizations would actually be strengthened by such joint efforts.

It would be extremely short-sighted for people to zero in on one aspect or another of existing civil rights groups and use it as an excuse for withholding support. All Americans, white and black, whatever their feelings about personalities or about specific stands on specific issues, must realize that these organizations have essential tasks to perform. They can only be effective if they get community support, so that they can speak from positions of strength. And they must have victories, if we are to keep the revolution for human rights in the hands of responsible leadership.

Black Americans have a special responsibility to become a truly unified community, capable of competing and of creating an Open Society. In the words of W. E. B. DuBois, ". . . we must strive by race organization, by race solidarity, by race unity to the realization of that broader humanity which freely recognizes the differences in men, but sternly deprecates inequality in their opportunities of development."

Pride is essential to this endeavor, and I think it extraordinary that we, who have for all our lives had it drummed into us that we were inferior, who have suffered under a caste system sanctified by custom and by law, have been able to develop a new, strong sense of pride. But it is important that our pride be in black *accomplishment*, not just in blackness or in antiwhiteness.

Black is beautiful when it is a slum kid studying to enter college, when it is a man learning new skills for a new job, or a slum mother battling to give her kids a chance for a better life. But white is beautiful, too, when it helps change society to make our system work for black people also. White is ugly when it oppresses blacks—and so is black ugly when black people exploit other blacks. No race has a monopoly on vice or virtue, and the worth of an individual is not related to the color of his skin.

Black people have a responsibility to organize the black community and then to work together with concerned white people to build an Open Society, free of racism, free of poverty.

We have come to the end of one era and the beginning of another. We are now in the post-civil-rights period. It is no longer a question of legal rights, but of whether White America will share political and economic power with Black America—and whether America itself will survive. Unless black demands for justice are met, our polarized society will find itself on a course of repression that will destroy the foundations of democracy. Yes, it *can* happen here.

If America is really serious about freedom and equality, it will have to prove that by allowing black people to be free and to be equal. That means that America must share with black people the power and the privileges now held only by white Americans. It cannot ask the black man to be responsible without giving him the responsibility for his own destiny; it cannot ask him to exercise discipline unless it allows him the power to control his own life.

The racism that pervades our society and influences the behavior of individuals and institutions alike must yield to the demands for justice and freedom. Together, blacks and whites can move our country beyond racism and create for the benefit of all of us an Open Society, one that assures freedom, justice, and full equality for all.